SOLOMON SCHECHTER

SOLOMON SCHECHTER

M.A., Litt.D.

A Bibliography

BY

ADOLPH S. OKO

CAMBRIDGE

AT THE UNIVERSITY PRESS

1938

CAMBRIDGE
UNIVERSITY PRESS

University Printing House, Cambridge CB2 8BS, United Kingdom

Cambridge University Press is part of the University of Cambridge.

It furthers the University's mission by disseminating knowledge in the pursuit of education, learning and research at the highest international levels of excellence.

www.cambridge.org
Information on this title: www.cambridge.org/9781107536609

First published 1938
First paperback edition 2015

A catalogue record for this publication is available from the British Library

ISBN 978-1-107-53660-9 Paperback

To

THE MEMORY OF
FRANK ISAAC SCHECHTER

TABLE OF CONTENTS

PREFATORY NOTE

THE aim in the subjoined record of the writings of Dr Solomon Schechter was "absolute" completeness, an ideal seldom or never achieved and but rarely approached. No such attempt was made as regards the Appendix. The list was prepared by me in the winter of 1915–16, soon after the death of the scholar, for inclusion in the Solomon Schechter Memorial Number of the *Hebrew Union College Monthly*. However, its publication there and then did not prove feasible; only the Preface, now much abridged and entirely rewritten, appeared in that journal. For various reasons, the work was laid aside and not taken up again until the summer of 1935. Some material was added in the meantime, and the whole recast. A number of titles were put before my notice by Professor Alexander Marx, of the Jewish Theological Seminary in New York. To him, too, I am indebted for helpful criticism at the early stage of the work—for all of which I render grateful thanks. It is also my pleasing duty to pay an old debt of gratitude to my former Secretary, Miss Sarah Belle Grad (now Mrs Moses Ades, of Louisville, Kentucky), for much help in connection with the initial preparation of the list. Finally, it would be a failure in gratitude not to mention the name of Rabbi Solomon Goldman of Chicago; my debt to him is very great.

The material here gathered is ordered under chronologically arranged dates forming headings, thus: (1) separate works; (2) contributions to the works of others and to collections; (3) articles in periodicals—irrespective of their being studies, reviews of books, "communications", etc.—arranged alphabetically under

the names of the periodicals, the articles themselves
following each other in the order of their appearance.
Reprints of a given article follow the entry; the title,
if not changed, is not repeated. They are provided with
sub-numerals, but are counted as separate items if new
matter has been added to their re-publication in book
form. Translations, regardless of their date of publication, follow the original. Reviews or criticisms of a
work listed follow that work, and, if signed, are arranged
alphabetically under the names of the reviewers; anonymous reviews precede those signed. No apology is
necessary for the inclusion of communications to the
Press, remarks on papers read at the Jews' College
Literary Society, testimonials or congratulatory letters.
These chips from the scholar's workshop may help to
round the one or the other of his essays or articles into
completeness. They are, besides, full of autobio-
graphical parentheses.

Notes accompany most of the entries. Their purpose
is to group and bring together scattered details into
some sort of orderly arrangement. They are bibliographical in nature, and represent a bibliographer's
effort to co-ordinate his material and thus add perhaps
to the usefulness of the list. Quotations from a book or
article described are often given. These serve to in-
dicate the contents of an entry, or else to illustrate the
author's point of view. They are not intended as
"samples" of erudition. Press notices of his publications are also recorded. They may be interesting as a
piece of *Culturgeschichte* of the time. The Jewish scholar
had a "good Press". In the field of Jewish learning
nothing like it, or similar to it, has happened before or
since.

The Appendix was not contemplated at first. Doubt-
less, there is more material scattered in periodicals and

newspapers touching upon Dr Schechter's career than was available, or readily accessible to me at the time of its redaction; but it is not likely that important articles have been overlooked. Here the alphabetical order could be maintained only in Section I. The arrangement of Section II and its more or less overlapping divisions is chronological.

The Index is quite full, and comprises in a single alphabet entries of names and topics.

Lastly, that this record of Dr Schechter's writings bears the imprint of the Press of his (adoptive) Alma Mater, will be a source of no little gratification to the circle of those who cherish his memory.

A. S. O.

August 1938

[The following abbreviations may be noted here:

Am. Heb.	*American Hebrew* (New York; weekly).
J.C.	*Jewish Chronicle* (London; weekly).
J. Comment	*Jewish Comment* (Baltimore; weekly).
J. Exponent	*Jewish Exponent* (Philadelphia; weekly).
J.P.S.A.	Jewish Publication Society of America.
J.Q.R.	*Jewish Quarterly Review* (old series, London; new series, Philadelphia).
J. Standard	*Jewish Standard* (London; weekly).
J.T.S.A.	Jewish Theological Seminary of America.
M.G.W.J.	*Monatsschrift für Geschichte und Wissenschaft des Judentums* (Breslau).
R.E.J.	*Revue des Études Juives* (Paris; quarterly).
Z.A.W.	*Zeitschrift für die Alttestamentliche Wissenschaft.*
Z.D.M.G.	*Zeitschrift der Deutschen Morgenländischen Gesellschaft.*

Other abbreviations explain themselves.]

SOLOMON SCHECHTER:
AN ESSAY*

IN the foremost rank of Jewish scholars of his day stood Solomon Schechter (1847?–1915). The great modern exponent of rabbinic teaching did not himself inaugurate the study of post-Exilic and Talmudical theology. The foundations of its critical treatment had already been laid, and its investigation had been fitfully pursued for some decades by Jewish and Christian scholars—as an independent entity by the former, and as an appanage to Christianity by the latter. Nor did he produce comprehensive systematic treatises, or standard works of ready reference. Rather, keen perception and profound spiritual insight were the marks of his special genius; and his *Studies in Judaism* and *Aspects of Rabbinic Theology*—remarkable equally for their great learning, their aphoristic wisdom and arresting literary qualities—have retained the authority of classics. Schechter's fame, however, does not rest on his books alone. In personality also he towered above his compeers. He had a sparkling, even a malicious wit, and a caustic humour. He was a man of many moods and not a few idiosyncrasies. He could scowl and hate like Carlyle, and laugh and love like Voltaire. But he had a stubborn philosophy of life, and one could always tell on which side he stood. There was the magic of revelation about the man—an elusive and

* First published in *The Menorah Journal*, Vol. **xxv**, No. 2 (April–June, 1937); now revised and somewhat enlarged.

mysterious object of the biographer's interest. We shall
not pursue it or attempt to resolve it. The stray strands
of character will not yield up the "secret".

Solomon Schechter was no intellectual Melchizedek.
In the annals of learning the scholar will be provided
with an intellectual pedigree, lineal and collateral. His
paternity will be fixed on his teachers, Meir Friedmann
and Isaac Hirsch Weiss, with N. Krochmal, Leopold
Zunz, J. L. Rapoport, M. Steinschneider and Abraham
Geiger as godfathers. Schechter did not hail from a
new and unexpected quarter. He came from the
Yeshibah—the scholastic hinterland that surrendered
its best minds to the *Haskalah*, the New Jewish Learning, and the university. During his early maturity,
however, Friedmann was the dominating influence.
Perhaps he was never displaced by any one. In any
case, his influence was decisive in setting the young
brilliant *Maskil*, who was flirting with satire and parody,
to work on Hebrew manuscripts. Henceforth he
dreams of variants and interpolations.

We know nothing of his youth, and but little of his
early studies. Schechter, we surmise, was never young.
He began to live fifteen years earlier than other men;
or, in another sense, he began to live fifteen years later
than other men. He had no mother-country. For to
be born a Jew in Rumania was to be born in void space.
The *Bahur* may have been a miracle of learning, but
his studies were not systematic. He early attained intellectual maturity; but he was hardly an all-informed
man of culture. There was nothing of the outstanding
author or editor in his start. And he was advanced in
years before he became an influence.

It was in England—whither he came, by fragile
chance, in 1882, by way of Vienna, by way of Berlin—
that Schechter found his opportunity: a grateful en-

vironment, a more or less secure home, and a congenial companion. Not that the satirical mocker and intellectual spendthrift became complaisant or contented. The personal incorporation of the scholar-gypsy into the safe and normal London Jewish community of the time was never complete. In truth, he did not want to be respectable, as yet. But his coming to England was the central incident of his life, and it coloured his whole thought. John Keble was soon joined to Moses Nahmanides and Mark Pattison was added to Nachman Krochmal. Not a little of Schechter's ideals and over-beliefs runs on a logic of personal and spiritual traits, qualities, and relations manifest in English religious thought of the latter half of the nineteenth century; they are not to be sought for alone in Hasidism and Maimonides. Schechter felt the after-effects of the Oxford Movement and of the *Essays and Reviews* not less than did Mr Claude G. Montefiore. Both seized their fighting terms from the arsenal of English thought, tradition and society, in addition to those taken from the repository of the Jewish past. "Catholic Israel", like "Liberal Judaism", has an English ring. The analogous facts in English society are easily recognizable. "Low Synagogue"—"High Synagogue"—"Universal Synagogue": these notions were not conceived in the Jewish communities of Lemberg, Vienna, Berlin, or Safed; they are, logically and theologically, of Oxford and Cambridge ancestry. Not that Schechter's Judaism was therefore less Judaeo-centric. But he was wont to insist that Jews should write their own (theological) love-letters, even if they did it badly....

To resume. Schechter soon uses the English tongue with rare felicity. The Jewish scholar—rare event!—can address himself both to the specialist and the general reader. He wins the reputation of great learning.

He obtains the post of Lecturer, and soon that of Reader, in Rabbinics at the University of Cambridge. He travels. He investigates. He makes discoveries. The English Press acclaims his great, and even romantic, finds. He conquers fame. He is titled Magister—yea, Doctor even. He is appointed Professor of Hebrew at University College, London. He is surrounded by erudite and congenial companions. True, he differs from them fundamentally; in norm and form, in training and mode of living they hail from different races, different religions, different societies. Cambridge, however, marked another important cycle in his life history. Here he became a revered—never a detached—authority. Here his social mien was fixed. In Cambridge Schechter became conscious of his powers.

His mode of thought was already fully formed during his stay at London. Essay upon essay and study upon study poured out from his pen. They attracted wide attention also among Christian scholars and theologians in sympathy with history or with Jewish study, their subject-matter alone inviting all sorts of comparisons; for human history is one. The range and depth of his attainments touched both Jewish *Wissenschaft* and Jewish life: pre-Talmudic literature and sects, Talmud and Midrash, law and legend, history and liturgy, mysticism and ethics, Karaite polemics and Gaonic apologetics; the social life of the times of Ben-Sira; the communal life of the Egyptian Jews in the Gaonic period; the intellectual and spiritual activity of the Jews in Palestine in the sixteenth century; the domestic concerns of the German Jews in the seventeenth and eighteenth centuries; the theological notions of English Jewry at the close of the nineteenth century —a range extraordinary indeed.

The *Hasid* brought a warm glow to his theme, which gave his work vitality and a personal note. From the start Schechter discarded the whole apparatus of polysyllables. There is nothing officious about his introductions to the "outlandish" manuscripts which he edited; and there is nothing official about his essays and studies. He wrote as a rebellious apologist rather than in the submissive spirit of historical research: the Jew rebelled against being a problem: the Jewish scholar took the offensive. His writings, indeed, are essentially illuminative rather than systematic: they are studies and aspects—suggestive syntheses rather than elaborate demonstrations. Schechter is never timid in reaching conclusions, and never indefinite in his judgements. Even his mistakes are stimulating. He exposes cant, if he does not reveal "the truth". Facts are extolled or condemned; to merely state them does not suit his temperament. He always takes sides. He is not arbitrary; he is only "partial". But his partiality was not "politic"; it was not a part of a "system". He hated, above all, finality. There is a good deal in Schechter that belongs to the category of "Table Talk"—the mode of teaching of the Hasidic *Zaddik*. But, however eclectic his material, however tangential his direction, his Hasidism was *sui generis*. His personal idiom exerted perhaps more influence than his impersonal ideas.

Little philosophy and less science are mirrored in his work. Schechter's erudition was greater than his capacity for abstract thought. Nor is there discernible any change or development in his central ideas; but we perceive an ever greater awareness of their implications. Schechter was an intuitive thinker. His thought was not atomic, and he did not advance his argument step by step. He was no more a sharp theologian than

xvii

the philosophical essayist Ahad HaAm was an acute logician. Strictly critical or logical inference did not satisfy them. Ahad HaAm's deep concern was the thought, or idea, or *Tendenz* of the historical phenomenon called Judaism. Schechter was wholly solicitous about the Jewish Tradition, conceived and interpreted as a living instrument of the nation rather than in any sharply defined theological sense. Tradition was the collective national wisdom and virtue. Tradition was nation-bound. "The Synagogue was a part of the Nation, not the Nation a part of the Synagogue." The history of the Synagogue was a biography of Jewish ideals. Judaism was not a complete (Sinaitic) revelation, but a complex of ideas and tendencies which developed gradually. It was the achievement of the nation. Jewish history was the story of Jewish lives as much as the development of dogma and institutions. His preoccupation was the beauty and fragrance of the dedicated life. His biographical studies of Jewish worthies were also intended as an instrument of personal edification. He preferred the saint to the statesman, the pious scholar and the mystic to the man of action or legist—or, Midrash and Haggadah to Halakah and Novellae. He was at best in dealing with individuals and almost at worst in tracing the development of ideas. The most influential Jewish theologian of his day was and remained a *Hasid*.

Modern study, no doubt, involved him more or less in a struggle with orthodoxy—and perhaps also with himself. The conception of historical development is irreconcilable with the traditional idea of revelation. Concerning the Mosaic authorship of the Pentateuch Isaac M. Wise was more "traditional" than Schechter. Nevertheless, Schechter was self-consistent on the whole. Tradition was for the sake of life. The inheritor of that

tradition accepted its normal doctrines: they were wise
and of vital importance. He accepted much and discarded little of the ritual; the subtleties of the Rabbis
in the sphere of observance made for a fence around
Tradition. It was no prison wall. He loved it, and
would not distinguish between fundamental and non-
fundamental articles of "belief". The age-old hopes of
the nation were also a part of Tradition; hence his
later adherence to Zionism. As the promise of a
cultural and social unity of the nation, purged of
antisemitic and assimilationist pollution, Zionism
would help to preserve and enrich that depository of
the nation's achievement. To be sure, Schechter no
more succeeded in being "traditional" or conservative
in every particular thing than his erstwhile English
friends succeeded in being "liberal", or orthodox, in
every particular, or his subsequent American good
neighbours—"His Majesty's Opposition"—have succeeded in being "reform" in every particular. His own
pietism (in the ritual sense) was not perversity or
spite—he was not a צדיק להכעיס.

Schechter loved the old, yet was not averse to the
new. He wanted a reformation from within, without
schism—not a synthetic manufacture of old forms with
new. The Dreamer of the Ghetto was now dreaming of
a "Catholic Israel": he was to be its High-Priest. He
was not refractory to the discipline of prolonged and
exact research in his chosen field. But he had since felt
that the editing of texts did not fulfil his mission, and
he added studies in Jewish thought and ideals. He soon
found that speculative thinking, too, did not end what
he considered his duty. The Torah was not a legal or
historical document, to be interpreted and annotated,
but a moral and social force. Action was now in order.
He would add the peculiar task of leader. His English

(not Rumanian) individualism was not timid. But
English Jewry was standing still under the burden of
a Chief Rabbinate. American Jewry, on the other hand,
was surging. America should be his base of operation;
the Jewish Theological Seminary in New York should
be his tribune. Certainly, he must have an organization.
Organization is natural and necessary. The soul needs
a body.

The scene shifts from England to the United
States—from Cambridge to New York (1902). Schechter fascinates the public. He exercises no less an influence as a teacher than as a writer. His lectures and
addresses not only breathe enthusiasm for his subject
but inculcate a Jewish attitude towards life. He is
stimulating. His clear pointed comments produce the
desired effect. His observations lend themselves to
quotation. Students and public repay him with en-
thusiastic devotion. No figure among Jewish scholars
is thought more attractive than that of Solomon
Schechter. Jewish study has had more critical methods.
Scholars may prefer a Steinschneider, or a Bacher. But
Schechter reveals its living interest. He makes his
appeal to all Jews. He is the first great instructor of
the Jewish youth in America—as Ahad HaAm is that
of the Jewish youth in Russia—as Martin Buber was
to be that of the Jewish youth in Germany. Jewish
students at American universities feel that they have
discovered a fresh, living Judaism. Schechter's Conservative Judaism seems less complacent, and also less
dogmatic, than Reform Judaism, and his conception of
"Catholic Israel" less archaic than the "Mission" idea
which had fallen to pieces in the American scheme of
life. He gives them not formulas but ideas. Attempts
are made (by Dr J. L. Magnes and, later, by Dr M. M.
Kaplan) to translate his "Catholic Israel" into equivalent

terms of institutions and action. Schechter himself breathes new life into Jewish study. The Genizah becomes a programme for the work of his colleagues. He inspires some of his students with enthusiasm to enter the dusty world of "research". His epigrammatic phrases are seized upon alike by Conservative and Reform pulpits as fighting terms—supplanting the vocabularies of Benjamin Szold and Marcus Jastrow, of Isaac M. Wise and Kaufmann Kohler. Schechter makes Conservative Judaism fashionable among the Lords of Life in New York.

But—the "spiritual honeymoon" was soon at an end. The great teacher turned administrator. He exchanged the task that was intellectual and spiritual for one that was worldly and ecclesiastical. The religious mystic shaped pragmatic policies. Incidental problems absorbed his interest. Learned controversies gave way to parochial contentions. Orthodoxy or Reform; Synod or Congregationalism; the Compatibility of Zionism with Americanism—these were the burning questions. Solomon Schechter, willy-nilly, became involved in what he hated most: "red-tape and platform Judaism". And the noise of the battle was disturbing to him. No philosophical movement followed. The "school" of the new Hillel only reproduced his own opinions. Antagonisms flourished.

Fate is ironic. And the climax of irony is capped by the fact that the prophet of Catholic Israel was mourned in England as "the great American Rabbi".

In magnis voluisse sat est.

BIBLIOGRAPHY OF THE WRITINGS OF
SOLOMON SCHECHTER

1876

1. מלה דמתיקא כדובשא. (השחר. Wien, 1876. Vol. 7, pp. 383–390.)

Signed, Ḥisda bar Ḥisda. A satire on Ḥasidism, in imitation of Joseph Perl's *Megalleh Ṭemirin*. See Davidson, I., *Parody in Jewish Literature*, pp. 76 and 223 (no. 106).

1877

2. שיחות חני צנתרא דדהבא. (השחר. Wien, 1877. Vol. 8, pp. 324–327, 416–419, 460–463.)

Signed, *Yaḥaẓ ben Rahẓah*. A satire on the Ḥasidic Rabbi Baer Friedmann of Leovo, in imitation of J. Perl's *Megalleh Ṭemirin*. For a full description of the contents, see Davidson, I., *Parody in Jewish Literature*, pp. 74–76 and 253 (no. 341). About the authorship of nos. 1 and 2, see Nacht, J., in דואר היום, 1925, no. 178; Malachi, A. R., in הדואר, vol. 4, 1925, no. 27; Rivkind, I., *ib.* no. 31.

1881

3. Antisemitische Ethnografie. (*Neuzeit.* Wien, 1881. Jahrg. 21, pp. 24–25.)

Criticism of an article published in *Ausland*, 1880, no. 50, which purports to describe certain customs of the Transcaucasian Jews. S. quotes Saul Berlin's glosses כסא דהרסנא to the responsa בשמים ראש (1793) about the "Unzuverlässigkeit der Historiographen und der Ethnographen".

1885

4. [פירוש ר״ג מדות מרב סעדיה גאון עם הקדמה והערות מאת זלמן שעכטער]. Cod. Opp. Add. Quo. 163 .בית תלמוד) Cat. N. 2469 [rather 2496], 135 a. [Vienna, 1885.] Vol. 4, pp. 235–244.)

SOLOMON SCHECHTER

Dedicated to the memory of Nathaniel Montefiore. S.
definitely ascribes the work, preserved only in Hebrew translation by Nahum (ha-Maarabi?), to Saadia. The work has been
reissued by J. Müller, *Œuvres complètes de R. Saadia*, tom. 9,
pp. 73–83.

REVIEW

[ANONYMOUS.] Saadia Gaon on the thirteen Middoth.
(*J.C.* Jan. 2, 1885, p. 12.)

5. צוואות ה״ר יהודא בן הרא״ש ואחיו ה״ר יעקב בעה״ט לבניו.
העתיקן והוציאן לאור זלמן שעכטער. (בית תלמוד.
[Vienna, 1885.] Vol. 4, pp. 340–346, 372–379.)

MS. Almanzi, no. 236 (S. erroneously gives 226) in the
British Museum (Add. 27129; Margoliouth Catalogue, pt. 3,
pp. 471–486, no. 1081: XXIV–XXV). Margoliouth "only
noted the existence of a printed edition of the text...when this
description was already in type. The quotations given may,
however, serve to correct a number of small mistakes in the
otherwise commendable publication..." (p. 479, footnote).

5*a*. צוואות הרב יהודה בן הרא״ש ואחיו ה״ר יעקב בעל
הטורים, הוציאן לאור על פי כתב יד עם הגהות
והערות שלמה זלמן שעכטער. פרעסבורג, תרמ״ה.
[Pressburg: Löwy & Alkalay, 1885.] 19 pp.
8°.

REVIEWS

LOEB, I. [Review.] (*R.E.J.* tom. 13, 1886, pp. 138–139.)
NEUBAUER, A. Ethical literature of Jewish writers. (*J.C.*
Dec. 4, 1885, p. 12.)

6. Lector I. H. Weiss. (*J.C.* Feb. 27, 1885, p. 15.)
Letter to the editor; signed, S. S. An appreciation on the
occasion of I. H. Weiss' seventieth birthday.

7. CHOTZNER, JOSEPH. Hebrew poets during the
middle ages. (*J.C.* Dec. 25, 1885, p. 11.)

Report of paper read before the Jews' College Literary Society; S. discussed Moses Ibn Ezra, Judah ha-Levi, Solomon Ibn Gabirol and Saadia ben Joseph Kalonymos.

8. Über Israel Alnaqua's מנורת המאור. (*M.G.W.J.* Jahrg. 34, 1885, pp. 114–126, 234–240.)

Description of, and extracts from, a MS. (Neubauer Catalogue, no. 1312), as well as an appreciation of the author, who died at the stake in 1391.

9. On the study of the Talmud. (*Westminster Review*, vol. 123, [new ser., vol. 67], pp. 20–53.)

Published anonymously. In the main a criticism of Edersheim, A., Life and Times of Jesus the Messiah, *London*, 1883.

REVIEWS

[ANONYMOUS.] Literarische Nachrichten. (*Neuzeit.* Wien, 1885. Jahrg. 25, p. 55.)

NEUBAUER, A. On the study of the Talmud. (*J.C.* Jan. 30, 1885, p. 13.)

"My readers will allow me to be indiscreet by giving the names of the joint authors, they are Mr S. Schechter and Mr Claude Montefiore.... Mr Schechter has not yet acquired sufficient knowledge of the language for presenting his interesting subject in a popular form, and, moreover, to adapt his criticisms to English taste. This was the work of Mr Montefiore."

9a. —— (*In his* Studies in Judaism, ser. 3, pp. 143–193; notes, pp. 291–296.)

1886

10. FRIEDLAENDER, MICHAEL. The age and authorship of Ecclesiastes. (*J.C.* March 5, 1886, p. 11.)

Report of paper read before the Jews' College Literary Society; lecturer's explanation that the Talmudic statement בקשו לגנוז referred to books already admitted into the canon, discussed by S.

11. ABRAHAMS, ISRAEL. The rod of Moses, and its legendary story. (*J.C.* Nov. 19, 1886, p. 13.)

Report of paper read before the Jews' College Literary Society; remarks by S.

12. "St Paul from a Jewish point of view." (*J.C.* Nov. 19, 1886, p. 14.)

Criticism of an article under that title by S. M. Schiller-Szinessy in *Expositor*, Nov. 1886. Protests against the author's "practice of regarding the Talmud as existing for no other purpose than to supply parallel passages to the New Testament".

13. Maimonides, Milde und Geistesfreiheit in seinen Gutachten. (*Neuzeit*. Wien, 1886. Jahrg. 26, pp. 136–138, 144–145, 172–174.)

Lecture delivered at the Beth Hamidrasch, Vienna. The MS. was submitted for publication by A. Jellinek.

1887

14. מסכת אבות דרבי נתן בשתי נוסחאות: א) הנוסחא
המפורסמת בתיקון והגהה ע"פ הדוגמאות וכתבי יד
שונים. ב) נוסחא אחרת עתיקה בכתב יד והוזכרה
בקצת ספרים ולא נדפסה עדיין. עם הערות עליהן
בענין חילוף הגירסאות והדוגמאות בשני התלמודים
והמדרשים ואיזה באורים בדרך קצרה. ועם מבוא מדבר
בהשתלשלות המסכת הזאת וטיבה ושתי נוסחאותיה
וטיב הכ"י הנמצאים ממנה ומפרשיה. ונלח לזה ארבע
הוספות מכילות לקוטי נוסחאות מכ"י שונים והשמטות
ותיקונים... ושלשה מפתחות מפתח לפסוקי תנ"ך
ומפתח לפרקי אבות ומפתח השמות. מאת שניאור
זלמן שעכטער. ווינא, תרמ"ז. Aboth de Rabbi
Nathan; hujus libri recensiones duas collatis
variis apud bibliothecas et publicas et privatas
codicibus edidit, prooemium notas appendices

4

indicesque addidit Salomon Schechter. *Londini: D. Nutt; Vindobonae: C. D. Lippe; Francofurti: J. Kauffmann,* 1887. xxxvi, 176 pp., 2l. 8°.

Printed in Vienna at the expense of the editor by M. Knöpflmacher. Dedicated to Claude G. Montefiore.

The current text as printed in the editions of the Talmud is revised by the aid of *codex* Oxford, *codex* Epstein, and of quotations. The revised text and a second recension "which has hitherto existed only in Manuscript [so far as was known to S., only in a Vatican MS. (Assemani Catalogue, no. 303); from a Munich MS. S. Taussig published a part in his *Neweh Shalom* (1872)], are printed in opposite columns. In the notes I have pointed out the parallel passages to either recension. A somewhat elaborate introduction seeks to explain the genesis of the tractate, its relation to contemporary Rabbinic literature, and the character of the MSS. The copious notes and appendices are intended to supply the student with helpful material towards a better understanding of the text." Short notice upon the issue of the first sheet in *J.C.* July 3, 1885, p. 5. S. is advised to append "a full list of the numerous abbreviations which he employs in his footnotes"; he heeded the advice, and added a short list of uncommon abbreviations. Short notice also in *Neuzeit*, Jahrg. 25, 1885, p. 246.

REVIEWS

[Anonymous review.] (*Athenaeum* [London], July 30, 1887, p. 146.)

[ANONYMOUS.] Mr Schechter's new work. (*J.C.* May 20, 1887, p. 12.)

[BRUELL, N.] Recension. (*Jahrbücher für jüdische Geschichte und Litteratur*, Jahrg. 9, 1889, pp. 133–139.)

FRIEDLAENDER, M. [Review.] (*Academy* [London], vol. 32, 1887, pp. 426–427.)

K[AUFMANN, D.?] Recension. (*M.G.W.J.* Jahrg. 36, 1887, pp. 374–383.)

N[EUBAUER], A. Bibliographie. (*R.E.J.* tom. 14, 1887, pp. 293–294.)

15. Rabbi Nachman Krochmal and the "Perplexities of the time". A paper read before the Jews' College Literary Society, Jan. 23, 1887. (*J.C.* Feb. 4, 1887, p. 11; Feb. 11, pp. 13–15.)

S.'s first lecture before an English audience, "but his delivery was clear and distinct". See *J.C.* Jan. 28, 1887, p. 13; see also Feb. 4, p. 9.

15*a*. —— London: "*Jewish Chronicle*" *Office*, 1887. 15 pp. 8°.

15*b*. —— (*In* Papers read before the Jews' College Literary Society during the session 1886. *London*, 1887. Pp. 68–80. 8°.)

The "Papers" were reviewed in *Academy* [London], April 1888.

15*c*. —— (*In his* Studies in Judaism, [ser. 1], pp. 46–72; notes, pp. 344–346.)

15*d*. Nachman Krochmal. Vortrag, gehalten in der "Litteraturgesellschaft des Jews' College" in London, am 23. Januar 1887. (*Populärwissenschaftliche Monatsblätter*. Frankfurt-a.-M., 1887. Jahrg. 7, pp. 83–96.)

The German version is much abridged.

16. Mr S. Schechter on the "Mechilta". (*J.C.* March 4, 1887, p. 13.)

A "somewhat compressed report" of an introductory lecture to a course of readings in Talmud and Midrash. The course continued for some time. See *J. Standard*, Jan. 4, 1889, p. 9 ("Mr Schechter and the Talmud", by J.K.L., who regrets "the disrespect which Mr Schechter's remarks must create for the Talmud"), and Jan. 18, p. 10 (criticism by A. Snowman, asserting that "Mr Schechter has not the remotest idea of the meaning of the study of the Talmud").

16*a*. The "Mechilta". From a lecture before the Jews' College, London. (*Hebrew Standard* [New York], March 25, 1887, p. 6.)

17. The Chassidim. A paper read before the Jews' College Literary Society. (*J.C.* Nov. 18, 1887, pp. 14–16; Nov. 25, pp. 14–15; Dec. 2, pp. 14–16.)

English translation (apparently from the German) by C. G. Montefiore. See *J.C.* Nov. 18, 1887, p. 9.

17*a*. —— London: "*Jewish Chronicle*" *Office*, 1887. 22 pp. 8°.

Dedication: "In affectionate memory of my friend the late Dr P. F. Frankl, Rabbi in Berlin."

17*b*. —— (*In his* Studies in Judaism, [ser. 1], pp. 1–45; notes, pp. 341–343.)

17*c*. Die Chassidim. Eine Studie über jüdische Mystik. [Aus dem Englischen übersetzt von Olga Tausig.] *Berlin: Jüdischer Verlag*, 1904. 93 pp., 3 l., 1 port. 12°.

17*d*. Die Chassidim. Autorisirte Uebersetzung von Marie Landmann. (*Nord und Süd.* Breslau, 1905. Bd. 112, pp. 83–111.)

17*e*. Chassidimii. Un studiu asupra misticismului judaic. Traducere de Baruch Zosmer. Cu o biografie a autorului de Dr J[acob] Nacht. [*Bucureşti*]: *Editura Asociaţiei Tineretului Intelectual Evreiesc diu România*, 1910. 64 pp. 16°. (Biblioteca "Hatikvah", no. 3.)

18. Le Midrasch Tanhuma et extraits du Yélamdénu et de petits Midraschim (fin) [par A. Neubauer]. (*R.E.J.* tom. 14, 1887, pp. 92–113.)

Pp. 95–101: מדרש תרי עשר (par Makhir?); MS. Harley 5704 (Margoliouth Catalogue, pt. 2, p. 3, no. 342): "Nous devons ces extraits à M. Schechter." Also pp. 111–113: "Voici les renvois des passages de Yélamdénu qu'on trouve dans d'autres Midraschim et ailleurs. Nous devons ce travail à l'obligeance de M. S. Schechter."

1888

19. The Graetz jubilee volume. (*J.C.* Jan. 6, 1888, p. 12.)

Signed, S.S. Review of Jubelschrift zum siebzigsten Geburts-tage des Prof. Dr H. Graetz, *Breslau*, 1887.

20. ADLER, M. David Alroy. (*J.C.* Jan. 6, 1888, p. 16).

Report of paper read before the Jews' College Literary Society; remarks by S.

21. [The reading of the Law.] (*J.C.* Jan. 13, 1888, p. 6.)

Letter to the editor; concerning the introduction of the triennial cycle of the reading of the Law in the Berkeley Street Synagogue, London. Avows to be "only interested in the interpretation of the passage in Megilla 29 *a*".

22. SIMMONS, L. M. [Maimonides and Islam.] Discussion on Maimonides and a personal messiah. (*J.C.* Jan. 13, 1888, p. 9.)

Report of paper read before the Jews' College Literary Society; discussion by S.

23. The belief in a personal messiah. (*J.C.* Jan. 27, 1888, pp. 6–7.)

Letter to the editor; referring to a correspondent, X.Y.Z. "I confess that I am not clear about many points in Jewish Eschatology....I wish only to speak a few words on behalf of the poor Rabbis, whom your learned correspondent did not mind abusing a little by the way."

—— X.Y.Z. The belief in a personal messiah. [A rejoinder.] (*J.C.* Feb. 3, 1888, p. 7.)

24. The "Baalshem"—Dr Falk. (*J.C.* March 9, 1888, pp. 15–16.)

Hayyim Samuel Jacob Falk's Diary (Neubauer, Catalogue of the Heb. MSS. in Jews' College, no. 127) and Jacob Emden's references to the author are the subject of the study. "To Professor Schechter belongs the merit of having discovered the connection between Falk and Sabbattianism" (H. Adler, "The Baal Shem of London", in *Transactions of the Jewish Historical Society of England,* [vol. 5], p. 153).

24 *a.* Der Baalschem Dr Falk. (*Jüdisches Litteratur-Blatt.* Magdeburg, 1888. Jahrg. 17, nos. 17–18.)

25. Notes on Anglo-Jewish history. I. גורניש—not Norwich. (*J.C.* May 4, 1888, p. 14.)

Refutes the theory of H. Adler (*The chief rabbis of England*) that "Gornish" is a corruption of "Norwich"; maintains that it is a corruption of "Mayence". "What led me to take up this subject was a desire to describe a MS. in the British Museum in which I have discovered many long extracts from the 'Tossafoth Gornish'."

—— LEVY, N. The existence of Tossafists of Norwich and York. (*J.C.* May 11, 1888, p. 9.)
Takes issue with S.

—— NEUBAUER, A. Dreux et Gournay. (*R.E.J.* tom. 17, 1888 [see pp. 156–157].)

26. Publications of the "Mekitze Nirdamim" Society. (*J.C.* May 11, 1888, p. 15.)

The works reviewed are A. Harkavy's edition of תשובות הגאונים; the ספר הגלוי, edited by H. J. Mathews; and the "Sammelband kleiner Beiträge aus Handschriften", vol. 3.

27. Gornish *not* Norwich. (*J.C.* May 18, 1888, pp. 5–6.)

Reply to N. Levy.

—— LEVY, N. The pre-expulsion rabbis of England and
Rabbenu Tam. [A rejoinder.] (*J.C.* May 25, 1888,
p. 6.)

28. A plea for the study of Hebrew literature. (*J.C.*
May 25, 1888, p. 13.)

29. The "Tossafoth-Gornish". II. (*J.C.* June 8,
1888, p. 16.)

Further details concerning the extracts in British Museum
MS. Add. 26965 (Margoliouth Catalogue, pt. 2, p. 73, no.
438). On "examining these quotations a little closer...I...
concluded that they must already have been printed, though
under a different title.... I found indeed that the much discussed Tossafoth-Gornish, or at least a part of them, were more
than two centuries ago published in the 'Novellae' (חירושים)
of R. Moses Galante on Jebamoth. The rarity of the book
makes a few descriptive words desirable." (See Benjacob, *Ozar
ha-Sefarim*, p. 559, no. 131 and p. 176, no. 292.)

30. Two historical works. (*J.C.* Aug. 3, 1888, p. 12.)

Review of Graetz, Heinrich, Volkstümliche Geschichte der
Juden, Bd. 1, *Leipzig*, 1888; Guedemann, Moritz, Geschichte
der Erziehungswesens und der Cultur der abendländischen
Juden..., vol. 3, *Wien*, 1888.

31. "Targum Onkelos." (*J.C.* Aug. 10, 1888, p. 12.)

Signed, S.S. Review of Schefftel, Simon Baruch, באורי אונקלוס,
München, 1888.

32. The Hebrew collection of the British Museum.
Articles 1–2. (*J.C.* Oct. 5, 1888, p. 13; Nov.
2, pp. 12–13.)

32 a. —— (*In his* Studies in Judaism, [ser. 1], pp.
252–269; notes, p. 357.)

32 *b.* Die Hebraica in der Bibliothek des British Museum. Übersetzt von L. Cohen. (*Jüdisches Litteratur-Blatt.* Magdeburg, 1888. Jahrg. 17, pp. 177–178, 182–183, 185–187, 189–190, 194–195.)

33. JACOBS, JOSEPH. [Jewish diffusion of folk-tales.] (*J. Standard,* May 11, 1888, pp. 3–4.)

Report of paper read before the Jews' College Literary Society; remarks by S.

34. A protest against personalities. (*J. Standard,* Nov. 2, 1888, p. 8.)

Letter to the editor; defence of S. Singer in the controversy about his proposal to introduce the reading of passages from the English Bible in synagogue service.

—— OPPENHEIM, S. The protest against personalities. [A reply.] (*J. Standard,* Nov. 9, 1888, p. 8.)

35. A contradiction. (*Jewish World* [London], Dec. 28, 1888, p. 3.)

Letter to the editor; repudiates the charges of plagiarism brought against him by S. M. Schiller-Szinessy in a review (*Jewish World,* Dec. 1, 1888, p. 3) of two articles by A. Neubauer (*R.E.J.* tom. 17, pp. 66–73, 154–157), for the first of which S. had copied a passage from the Mahzor Vitry MS. in the British Museum. S. is accused of having copied the passage from an unpublished catalogue by Charles Taylor, and not from the original; also of having appropriated from plaintiff the discovery that Rashi was already called "Jarchi" by Raymundus Martini in his *Pugio Fidei.* The controversy continued for some time in the *Jewish World* under the heading "Dr Schiller-Szinessy and Mr Schechter": Jan. 4, 1889, p. 3, S.-Sz. reiterates the charge; Jan. 11, p. 3, S. Singer defends S.; Jan. 18, p. 3, S.-Sz. replies; Feb. 1, p. 3, Singer rejoins; Feb. 15, p. 3, S.-Sz. comes back to the charge; Feb. 22, p. 3, A. Neubauer answers accusations levelled against him, and also defends S.;

11

March 1, p. 3, S.-Sz. repeats the attack; March 8, p. 3, Neubauer retorts; March 15, p. 3, S.-Sz. returns once more to his accusations—when, finally, the editor closed the correspondence. See also: *J. Standard*, March 1, 1889 (comment by Marshallik, *i.e.* I. Zangwill). Apparently, S.-Sz. was paying off old scores. Neubauer had criticized S.-Sz.'s article on the Midrash (*Encyclopaedia Britannica*, 9th ed.) in a review of S.'s "On the study of the Talmud" (no. 9); he also took issue with him in "Raymundus Martini and the Rev. Dr Schiller-Szinessy" (*Academy*, 1887). For S.'s animadversion see no. 12.

1889

36. In memoriam [Asher Asher]. (*J.C.* Jan. 11, 1889, p. 8.)

36 a. —— (*In* Asher, Asher, Some notes and articles by the late A. Asher...with reprints of his newspaper obituaries.... [*London*], 1916. Pp. 182–184. 8°.)

37. Targum on Isaiah. (*J.C.* Jan. 25, 1889, p. 17.)

Review of Lewis, Harry S., Targum on Isaiah i–v; with (Hebrew) commentary, *London*, 1889.

38. Titles of books. (*J.C.* June 21, 1889, pp. 14–16.)

—— IMBER, N. H. Title-pages. [Discussion of above.] (*J. Standard*, June 28, 1889, p. 3.)

Reads: "To be continued"; but no more appeared.

38 a. Titles of Jewish books. (*In his* Studies in Judaism, [ser. 1], pp. 270–281; notes, p. 357.)

39. The dogmas of Judaism. (*J.Q.R.* vol. 1, 1889, pp. 48–61, 115–127.)

An outline of the history of Jewish dogmas. See also *J. Standard*, Jan. 25, 1889, p. 8.

39 a. —— (*In his* Studies in Judaism, [ser. 1], pp. 147–181; notes, pp. 351–353.)

1890

40. Application and testimonials for the post of lecturer in Talmudic in the University of Cambridge. [*London: Wertheimer, Lea and Co.*], 1890. 12 pp. 12°.

Application, addressed "To the Vice-Chancellor of the University of Cambridge", comprises pp. 3–4; the testimonials are by H. Adler, W. Bacher, T. K. Cheyne, S. R. Driver, J. Freudenthal, H. Graetz, A. Jellinek, I. Levy, A. Neubauer, A. H. Sayce, M. Steinschneider and I. H. Weiss.

40*a*. —— [*London: Wertheimer, Lea and Co.*], 1890. 18 pp. 12°.

Contains additional testimonials by N. Bruell, M. Friedmann, R. J. H. Gottheil, M. Guedemann, S. J. Halberstam, D. Kaufmann, S. Maybaum and D. Rosin.

41. Rabbinic parallel to a story of Grimm. (*Folk-lore*, vol. 1, 1890, pp. 277–278.)

"In preparing my edition of the Great Midrash on the Pentateuch...I came across the following, which my friend Mr Jacobs thinks would be of interest to students of folk-lore." According to J. Jacobs, the story is a variant of Grimm's "The two travellers".

42. The riddles of Solomon in rabbinic literature. (*Folk-lore*, vol. 1, 1890, pp. 349–358.)

Hebrew text, English translation, introductory and explanatory remarks; edited "for the first time from the *Midrash Hachephez* [מדרש החפץ], existing only in Yemen MSS., of which the British Museum has four copies....Our copy is prepared from Or. 2382 [Margoliouth Catalogue, pt. 2, p. 26, no. 365]. The MSS. vary very little, and the only essential variation we found we have inserted in its place." The compiler, the physician Yahya ibn Suleiman (or Zechariah ben Solomon), "wrote as late as 1430", but "the late age...would not prove much against the antiquity of his version of the legend". See *J.C.* Oct. 3, 1890, p. 6.

13

43. The beginnings of the Hagadah. (*J.C.* Jan. 24, 1890, p. 19.)

Review of BACHER, WILHELM. Die Agada der Tanaiten, *Strasburg*, 1884–90, 2 vols.

44. [Eulogy on Chief Rabbi N. M. Adler; report of the meeting of the Jews' College Literary Society.] (*J.C.* Feb. 14, 1890, p. 10.)

45. Rabbi Elijah Wilna, Gaon. A paper read at Jews' College, Feb. 9, 1890. (*J.C.* Feb. 14, 1890, pp. 14–15; Feb. 21, p. 12; Feb. 28, p. 19.)

See also Feb. 14, p. 6 and Feb. 21, p. 8.

—— COHEN, L. The exact date of the Gaon's death. (*J.C.* March 7, 1890, p. 8.)

Fixes date as Oct. 9, 1797, the 5th day of Sukkot, not the 3rd, as stated by S.

45 a. Mr Schechter on the Wilna Gaon. (*J. Standard*, Feb. 14, 1890, p. 4.)

Report of paper; a much abridged version. See also p. 7 (editorial comment).

45 b. Rabbi Elijah Wilna, Gaon.... *London: "Jewish Chronicle" Office*, 1890. 12 pp. 8°.

45 c. Der Gaon von Wilna. (*Jüdisches Litteratur-Blatt*. Magdeburg, 1890. Jahrg. 19, pp. 42–43.)

"Nach dem Jewish Stand[ard]."

45 d. Rabbi Eliah Wilna Gaon. Vortrag gehalten in der literarischen Gesellschaft des "Jews [!] College" am 9. Februar 1890. Uebersetzt von Ignatz Kaufmann. *Wien: Verlag d. "Oesterreichischen Wochenschrift"*, 1891. 24 pp. 8°.

BIBLIOGRAPHY

46. Jewish homiletics. (*J.C.* Aug. 15, 1890, p. 11.)
Review of Maybaum, S., Jüdische Homiletik, *Berlin*, 1890.

47. The child in Jewish literature. (*J.Q.R.* vol. 2, 1890, pp. 1–24.)
Paper read before the Jews' College Literary Society, Dec. 23, 1888. See *J.C.* Dec. 28, 1888, pp. 11–12 (extensive report of paper and discussion). See also p. 5. It was "the late Miriam Harris, a friend of children...who had inspired him with the idea of choosing the subject".

47 *a*. —— (*In his* Studies in Judaism, [ser. 1], pp. 282–312; notes, pp. 358–359.)
The Jüdischer Verlag, Berlin, announced in 1904 "Schechter's Das Kind in der jüdischen Literatur" as ready for publication; but it did not appear.

48. A recent case of plagiarism. (*J.Q.R.* vol. 2, 1890, p. 108.)
Shows that the work דרכי ציון, edited by Zebi Ezekiel Michaelsohn (1886), was a literary piracy.

49. A Jewish Boswell. (*J.Q.R.* vol. 2, 1890, pp. 139–141.)
Deals with Solomon of St Goar and his master, Jacob ha-Levi (Maharil).

49 *a*. —— (*In his* Studies in Judaism, [ser. 1], pp. 142–146; notes, p. 351.)

50. Translation of the Talmud in England in 1568? (*J.Q.R.* vol. 2, 1890, pp. 188–189.)
Draws attention to a statement in the Hebrew preface to שלחן הפנים (Ladino: Mesa de el alma; S. erroneously gives לחם הפנים), Salonica, 1568 (also Venice, 1602), to the effect "that in England the Gentiles are now printing the Talmud in Latin". As S. points out, Steinschneider (Cat. Bodleiana, no. 6286: 1) already refers to this statement. (See also Benjacob, p. 588, no. 744.) [S. used the copy of Dr Louis

15

Loewe of London, and remarks: "Hitherto the Salonica edition was known only through one copy in the possession of the British Museum.... We have thus at present two copies of this rare work." The Library of the J.T.S.A. possesses a copy; so does Dr M. B. Amzalak of Lisbon. The van Biema Catalog (1904) notes a copy (no. 2738).]

51. Algazi's Chronicle and the names of Patriarchs' wives. (*J.Q.R.* vol. 2, 1890, p. 190.)

Shows that the enumeration of the names of the wives of Biblical personages in Samuel Algazi's תולדות אדם "agrees more or less with the Book of Jubilees".

52. The Rabbis of Lemberg. (*J.Q.R.* vol. 2, 1890, pp. 514–517.)

Review of Dembitzer, Hayyim Nathan, Klilath Jofi, enthaltend die Geschichte der Rabbiner der Stadt Lemberg... [Hebrew, vol. 1], *Krakau*, 1888.

53. A new Jewish novel. (*J.Q.R.* vol. 2, 1890, pp. 518–519.)

Review of Simon, Oswald John, The world and the cloister; a novel, *London*, 1890, 2 vols.

1891

54. The praying woman. A sketch. (*J.C.* Feb. 13, 1891, pp. 18–19.)

54a. Woman in temple and synagogue. (*In his* Studies in Judaism, [ser. 1], pp. 313–325; notes, p. 359.)

A few paragraphs omitted and a number of verbal changes made.

54b. Salomon Schechter: Die Frau in Tempel und in der Synagoge. [Von Isi Broch aus dem Englischen übersetzt.] (*Jude, Der*. Berlin, 1924. Jahrg. 8, pp. 523–530.)

55. The late Professor Graetz. (*J.C.* Sept. 18, 1891, pp. 8–9.)
Obituary.

56. The prospects of Jewish literature in England. (*J.C.* [Jubilee supplement], Nov. 13, 1891, pp. 20–21.)
Pleads for "a commentary to the Bible, on the scale of the Speaker's Commentary, but written from a Jewish point of view...a good translation of the Machzor, something on the scale of that of Sachs.... A popular history of Jewish literature is also a great desideratum, whilst a good Reader for schools has also to be written. We should like even to see a good novel written by some Jewish Kingsley, let us say, on 'economical' Judaism which would show that if there ever was a religion that regarded 'the world as the subject of redemption', it was the religion of the Old Testament." Article contains also brief characterizations of Dr A. Benisch, L. Dukes, J. Zedner, Rev. A. L. Green and Dr A. Asher.

57. The doctrine of divine retribution in rabbinical literature. (*J.Q.R.* vol. 3, 1891, pp. 34–51.)
Forms article III of a symposium on "The doctrine of divine retribution": I. The Old Testament, by C. G. Montefiore; II. The New Testament, by J. E. Odgers. "Judaism has no fixed doctrine on the subject."

57a. —— (*In his* Studies in Judaism, [ser. 1], pp. 213–232; notes, pp. 354–355.)

58. Jewish Literature in 1890. (*J.Q.R.* vol. 3, 1891, pp. 314–342.)
Critical survey; "...most of the books which are published in the East were quite inaccessible to me, and...many of those that have reached me belong... to a class of books which was already obsolete at the beginning of the century. They do not increase our stock of information on a single point, and serve only as a warning example of the uselessness of learning that does not submit to the control of a sound scientific method." A "Postscript" (pp. 338–342) reviews Ch. M. Horowitz's תוספתא עתיקתא.

59. The quotations from Ecclesiasticus in rabbinic literature. (*J.Q.R.* vol. 3, 1891, pp. 682–706.)

"The quotations... have been collected by various scholars... [but] have never been put together with full parallels, and the different readings which the MSS. and the older editions offer.... Besides, there are to be found some quotations of and parallels to Sirach in Rabbinical works, which have only been edited during the last few years.... In the present article an attempt will be made to supply this want."

60. The Law and recent criticism. (*J.Q.R.* vol. 3, 1891, pp. 754–766.)

A critique of Toy, C. H., Judaism and Christianity..., *London*, 1890.

60a. —— (*In his* Studies in Judaism, [ser. 1], pp. 233–251; notes, pp. 356–357.)

1892

61. Legal evasions of the Law. (*In* Montefiore, C. G., Lectures on the origin and growth of religion as illustrated by the religion of the ancient Hebrews. [The Hibbert Lectures, 1892.] *London*, 1892, pp. 557–563. 8°.)

Second edition, London, 1893; third edition, London, 1897.

Forms Appendix II. "The so-called 'Evasion Laws' in Rabbinical Judaism, to which reference is occasionally made in theological works, are very few in number." See *J.C.* Dec. 29, 1911, p. 21 (discussion of S.'s view). Montefiore's references to S.: p. 426 (footnote; on St Francis); pp. 506–508 (on Sabbath under the Law); p. 534 (footnote; on Ruskin and the Law). "To Mr Schechter I owe more than I can adequately express here. My whole conception of the Law and of its place in Jewish religion and life is largely the fruit of his teaching and inspiration, while almost all the Rabbinic material upon which that conception rests was put before my notice and explained to me by him" (*Preface*, p. x).

62. Doctrine and the United Synagogue. (*J.C.* July 8, 1892, pp. 5–6.)

Letter to the editor; defends Rev. Morris Joseph, whom Chief Rabbi H. Adler declared unfit for the ministry of one of his synagogues, pointing out that to make doctrines the test of the minister would be "unpractical", because "very few could stand it". He instances L. Zunz, H. Graetz, L. Herzfeld, M. Joel, G. Salomon. "I also frankly admit that I and many like me who follow the views indicated above with more or less consistency—just according to the conservative or liberal turn of mind of the follower—have no right to consider ourselves orthodox." See *J.C.* July 8, 1892, p. 11 (comment).

62a. —— (*Reform Advocate*. Chicago, 1892. Vol. 3, p. 566.)

63. Notes on Hebrew MSS. in the University Library at Cambridge. I. (*J.Q.R.* vol. 4, 1892, pp. 90–101.)

MSS. Add. 474. Description of (A) *Responses* of Isaiah of Trani, the elder; (B) *Responses* of the Geonim. See *J.C.* May 20, 1892, p. 6 ("Already the preparation of the catalogue of the Cambridge Hebrew MSS. has been more or less formally committed to his charge").

64. Notes on Hebrew MSS. in the University Library at Cambridge. II. (*J.Q.R.* vol. 4, 1892, pp. 245–255.)

MSS. Add. 434. Description of (A) Commentary to the prayers and benedictions, and (B) Commentary to the Haggadah for Passover by Judah ben Yakkar, the teacher of Nahmanides.

65. The history of Jewish tradition. (*J.Q.R.* vol. 4, 1892, pp. 445–470.)

Study of Weiss, I. H., Zur Geschichte der jüdischen Tradition, *Wien*, 1871–91, 5 vols. (Hebrew).

65a. —— (*In his* Studies in Judaism, [ser. 1], pp. 182–212; notes, pp. 353–354.)

2-2

66. Notes on Hebrew MSS. in the University Library at Cambridge. III. (*J.Q.R.* vol. 4, 1892, pp. 626–627.)

MS. Add. 426. Description of an anonymous commentary and glosses to the tractate *Moed Katon* of the Babylonian Talmud. "It is probably the fullest and most important commentary we possess to this Tractate....Our author must... have flourished in the first decade after the middle of the 13th century."

67. Notes sur Messer David Léon, tirées des manuscrits. (*R.E.J.* tom. 24, 1892, pp. 118–138.)

Extracts (1) from MS. Montefiore 465 (Hirschfeld Catalogue, no. 290), entitled מגן דוד; (2) from MS. Oxford (Neubauer Catalogue, no. 834; now כבוד חכמים, ed. S. Bernfeld, who, however, does not refer to S.; entry in Benjacob, p. 296, no. 501, needs correction).

1893

68. A visit to Rome. (*J.C.* Oct. 20, 1893, pp. 10–11.)

For notices about S.'s journey to Italy to examine Hebrew MSS., see *Appendix*, II, 2 (Italy). A full report of the journey on the Worts Studentship for foreign travel was made by S. in 1893 to the Vice-Chancellor of Cambridge University.

68 a. The earliest Jewish community in Europe. (*In his* Studies in Judaism, [ser. 1], pp. 326–340; notes, p. 359.)

69. Notes on Hebrew MSS. in the University Library at Cambridge. IV. (*J.Q.R.* vol. 5, 1893, pp. 18–23.)

MS. Dd. 5.38 [or Add. Do. 5, 38]. Description of the ספר המנהגות by Asher ben Saul. This work "must have been written after 1205, which I regard as the date when the author flourished". (According to the *Jewish Encyclopedia*, vol. 2, p. 184, he "lived in the fourteenth century".)

—— HALBERSTAM, S. J. Asher ben Saul and the Sefer Haminhagoth. (*J.Q.R.* vol. 5, 1893, pp. 350–351.)
Agrees with S.'s identification of the author as R. Asher ben Saul, and not as Asher ben Meshullam, according to H. J. Michael.

70. Nachmanides. (*J.Q.R.* vol. 5, 1893, pp. 78–121.)
Paper read before the Jews' College Literary Society, May 22, 1892. Confines himself "to those features and peculiarities ...which will illustrate Nachmanides the tender and compassionate, the Nachmanides who represented Judaism from the side of emotion and feeling, as Maimonides did from the side of reason and logic". See *J.C.* May 27, 1892, pp. 6 and 16 (report); Oct. 28, p. 6 (comment).

70a. —— (*In his* Studies in Judaism, [ser. 1], pp. 99–141; notes, pp. 347–350.)
MS. document given only in translation.

71. Notes on Hebrew MSS. in the University Library at Cambridge. V. (*J.Q.R.* vol. 5, 1893, pp. 244–245.)
MS. Add. 667, 3. Colophons by (1) Moses ben Nathanael, copyist, and (2) Joseph Chamiz (or Hamiz), owner. The two colophons "are not without a certain bibliographical as well as historical interest".

72. RYLE, HERBERT EDWARD. The canon of the Old Testament.... *London*, 1892. [Review of.] (*J.Q.R.* vol. 5, 1893, pp. 342–344.)
[S. intended to edit Joseph Zabara's "Book of Delight" in collaboration with I. Abrahams "one of these days". (See *J.C.* Aug. 4, 1893, p. 10.)]

1894

73. [Adolf Jellinek; obituary.] (*J.C.* Jan. 5, 1894, p. 8.)
Preceded by a tribute from I. Abrahams and followed by one from E. N. Adler.

73*a.* Adolf Jellinek. Ein Gedenkblatt von L. [!]
Schechter in Cambridge. Deutsch von Ignaz
Kaufmann. (*Oesterreichische Wochenschrift.*
Wien, 1894. No. 4, pp. 66–67.)

74. The Jews of Rome. I–II. (*J.C.* Aug. 3, 1894,
p. 13; Aug. 10, p. 13.)

Review of Berliner, Adolf, Geschichte der Juden in Rom von
der ältesten Zeit bis zur Gegenwart..., *Frankfurt-a.-M.*
1893, 2 vols.

75. [Lectures on rabbinic theology.] (*J.C.* Oct. 26,
1894, p. 12; Nov. 2, p. 8; Nov. 9, p. 9; Nov.
16, p. 20; Nov. 30, p. 13; Dec. 7, p. 15.)

Extensive reports of a course of six lectures on "Rabbinic
Theology, with especial reference to the doctrines discussed by
Paul the Apostle", delivered at University Hall, London, Oct.
24, 31; Nov. 7, 14, 28; Dec. 5. See *J.C.* July 20, 1894, p. 21
(announcement); Sept. 28, p. 16 ("Mr Schechter's forthcoming
lectures"); Oct. 26, pp. 11–12 ("A time to speak"; editorial
comment).

76. A Hebrew elegy. (*In* Jewish Historical Society of
England. Transactions. *London* [1894]. [Vol.
1], pp. 8–14. 4°.)

Description, together with Hebrew text and English translation, of the last ten stanzas of a *Kinah* (Vatican Library, *codex*
312) composed by Menahem b. Jacob b. Solomon b. Menahem,
bearing on Anglo-Jewish history. The *Jewish Encyclopedia*
(vol. 8, p. 467) gives the name as Menahem ben Jacob ben
Solomon ben Simon. See *J.C.* Nov. 17, 1893, p. 15 and Dec.
1, p. 17 (comments).

77. Notes on Hebrew MSS. in the University Library
at Cambridge. VI. (*J.Q.R.* vol. 6, 1894, pp.
136–145.)

MSS. Oo 1: 3, 4, 5, 16, 19, 20, 23, 24, 30, 32, 33, 34, 35,
37, 38, 42, 45, 46, 47, 48, 49, and Add. 271. Oo 1: 3, 4, 5 are
described in the Schiller-Szinessy Catalogue (nos. 1, 8, 10,

respectively). "This group of MSS., though of no great intrinsic value, deserves to be treated in these pages on account of the interest attaching to the place from which they come. They were presented to the University by the Rev. Claudius Buchanan, who brought them all from his travels on the coast of Malabar. . . . But though we are also told there [Buchanan, *Christian researches*] that he procured them from the Synagogue of the Black Jews, there is, if we except the New Testament MSS., nothing peculiar or sectarian about them, excluding them from the Synagogue of the White Jews."

78. Some aspects of rabbinic theology. I–II. (*J.Q.R.* vol. 6, 1894, pp. 405–427, 633–647.)

I. Introductory. II. God is far, but not remote. I corresponds with chap. 1 in book; II, including continuation, with chap. 11 (God and the world), 111 (God and Israel), 1v (Election of Israel), and v (The kingdom of God: invisible). See *J.C.* Jan. 19, 1894, p. 14 (announcement); March 30, p. 6; July 13, pp. 6–7; Jan. 15, 1895, p. 13 (comments).

79. Fragment of the Sifre Zuta [ספרי זוטא]. (*J.Q.R.* vol. 6, 1894, pp. 656–663.)

Edited from MS. Heb. c. 18 in the Bodleian Library (Neubauer-Cowley Catalogue, p. 30, no. 2634). See *J.C.* Nov. 3, 1893, p. 19 (I. Abrahams announces the discovery).

80. Agadath Shir Hashirim. (*J.Q.R.* vol. 6, 1894, pp. 672–697; vol. 7, 1895, pp. 145–163.)

Edited from the Parma MS. (*codex* De Rossi, no. 541).

[S.'s publications during 1894 are briefly commented upon in *J.C.* Sept. 28, 1894, p. 18.]

1895

81. Syllabus of a course of six lectures on rabbinic theology, delivered before the Gratz College. *Philadelphia*, 1895.

Delivered Feb. 11–28, 1895. Lecture I. The difficulties of the subject. . . . Lecture II. Surprise of the Jewish student at

the assertion of Christian theologians of the remoteness of the
Jewish God.... Lecture III. The kingdom of God in rabbinical
literature.... Lecture IV. The invisible kingdom of God....
Lecture V. The Torah as law in particular.... Lecture VI.
Sin.... "At a meeting of the committee held November 29,
1894, it was resolved that a series of lectures be given during the
year 1894–95, and that Mr S. Schechter...be invited to deliver
a number of lectures of this series." See Gratz College,
Publications (*Philadelphia*, 1897), [vol.] 1, p. 9. See also *Am.
Heb.* vol. 56 (1894–95), p. 320; *J.C.* Jan. 4, 1895, p. 16; Jan.
25, p. 18; March 1, p. 11; *J. Exponent*, issues of Feb. 1895.

82. [JACOBS, JOSEPH.] As others saw him: a retrospect
A.D. 54. *London*, 1895. [Review of.] (*J.C.*
May 10, 1895, p. 16; May 17, pp. 16–17.)

Signed, Azoi.

82 a. —— (*In his* Studies in Judaism, ser. 3, pp. 25–
46; notes, p. 279.)

Last sentence omitted.

83. Some aspects of rabbinic theology. III. (*J.Q.R.*
vol. 7, 1895, pp. 195–215.)

Corresponds, in book, with chaps. VI (The visible kingdom:
universal) and VII (The kingdom of God: national).

84. Corrections and notes to Agadath Shir Hashirim.
(*J.Q.R.* vol. 7, 1895, pp. 729–754; vol. 8,
1896, pp. 289–320.)

85. Seder Olam Suta [סדר עולם זוטא]. (*M.G.W.J.*
Jahrg. 39, 1895, pp. 23–28.)

Also off-print; without t.-p. Edited from the Parma MS.
(*codex* De Rossi, no. 541). "Den Inhalt des vorliegenden
Theiles des MS....habe ich...nicht genau studirt sodass ich
zu einem Urtheil über den Werth oder Unwerth desselben nicht
berechtigt bin." See *J.C.* Nov. 2, 1894, p. 15 (comment).

86. BUBER, SALOMON. Midrasch Suta.... *Berlin*,
1894. 8°. [Review of.] (*M.G.W.J.* Jahrg. 39,
1895, pp. 562–566.)

Differs but slightly from the English (no. 92).
[Of S.'s work under way in 1895, the *J.C.* (May 10, 1895,
p. 18) enumerates: Notes on *Agadath Shir Hashirim*; an instalment of the "Aspects"; essay on "Safed in the fifteenth
century"; "one or two other essays, lectures, etc.".]

1896

87. Studies in Judaism. By S. Schechter, M.A.,
Reader in Talmudic in the University of
Cambridge. *London: A. and C. Black* [also,
*Philadelphia: The Jewish Publication Society of
America*], 1896. xxv, 366 pp. 8°.

Contents: [Preface.] Introduction. 1. The Chassidim. 2.
Nachman Krochmal and the "Perplexities of the time".
3. Rabbi Elijah Wilna, Gaon. 4. Nachmanides. 5. A Jewish
Boswell. 6. The dogmas of Judaism. 7. The history of Jewish
tradition. 8. The doctrine of Divine retribution in rabbinical
literature. 9. The Law and recent criticism. 10. The Hebrew
collection of the British Museum. 11. Titles of Jewish books.
12. The child in Jewish literature. 13. Woman in temple and
synagogue. 14. The earliest Jewish community in Europe.
Notes. Index.

Dedication: "To the ever-cherished memory of the late
Dr P. F. Frankl, Rabbi in Berlin, these studies are reverently
dedicated." Excepting the Introduction, these studies first
appeared in *J.Q.R.* and *J.C.* They "have been written on
various occasions.... If some sort of unity may be detected in
the book, it can only be between the first three essays...in
which there is a certain unity of purpose.... Eight of these
essays are more or less of a theological nature." The ninth
essay is "a humble attempt [at] a subject which I have essayed
to expound in a series of essays on 'Some Aspects of Rabbinic
Theology'.... The last five essays touch rather on certain
social and familiar aspects of Judaism.... They are mere
causeries...." Issued May 8, 1896 (*J.C.* May 8, 1896,
p. 118). "So impressed was Dr Black with the merit of these

SOLOMON SCHECHTER

essays that he has already invited Mr Schechter to allow the firm to publish a second volume next season" (*J.C.* Oct. 4, 1895, p. 13); published in 1908. "A German translation of the volume is already in contemplation" (*J.C.* June 26, 1896, p. 19); not published. See *J.C.* Sept. 4, 1896, p. 17 (reference). Extracts: *J.C.* Dec. 29, 1907, p. 11 ("Conservative Judaism and modern thought"); Hertz, J. H., *A Book of Jewish Thoughts* (London, 1920; and translations). See also Greenberg, L. J., "A plea for a conference....An address..." (*J.C.* March 12, 1897, pp. 25–26).

REVIEWS

[ANONYMOUS.] Contribution to Biblical literature. (*Athenaeum.* London, 1896. July 18, p. 94.)

[ANONYMOUS.] Literature. (*Critic.* New York, 1897. Vol. 30, p. 352.)

[ANONYMOUS.] Literary reviews. (*Menorah.* New York, 1896. Vol. 21, pp. 64–65.)

BADT, [B.]. Besprechung. (*M.G.W.J.* Jahrg. 41, 1897, pp. 45–48.)

DODS, M. Studies in Judaism. (*Bookman.* New York, 1896–97. Vol. 4, pp. 70–71.)

ELLINGER, M. Schechter's Studies in Judaism. (*Am. Heb.* vol. 76, 1904–5, pp. 28–30.)

[HASTINGS, J.] Notes on recent exposition. (*Expository Times,* vol. 7, 1895–96, pp. 436–438.)

—— Notes on recent exposition. (*Expository Times,* vol. 8, 1896–97, pp. 1–3.)
Discusses the essay "Woman in temple and synagogue".

[HIRSCH, E. G.] Editorial note. (*Reform Advocate.* Chicago, 1896. Vol. 11, p. 279.)

JACOBS, J. [Review.] (*Young Israel.* London, 1898. Pp. 65–67, 90–91.)

JOSEPH, M. Mr Schechter's "Studies in Judaism". (*J.C.* May 15, 1896, pp. 22–23.)

MACALISTER, A. Critical notices. (*J.Q.R.* vol. 9, 1897, pp. 522–528.)

MOORE, G. F. Recent theological literature. (*American Journal of Theology,* vol. 1, 1897, pp. 183–186.)

SIEGFRIED, K. Das Judenthum. (*Theologischer Jahresbericht,* Bd. 16, 1896, p. 98.)

26

88. אגדת שיר השירים. Agadath Shir Hashirim; edited from a Parma manuscript, annotated and illustrated with parallel passages from numerous MSS. and early prints, with a post-script on the history of the work by S. Schechter, M.A., Reader in Rabbinic at the University of Cambridge. Reprinted from the "Jewish Quarterly Review". *Cambridge: Deighton Bell and Co.* [and] *London: George Bell and Sons,* 1896. 3 p. l., (1)4–112 pp. 8°.

Printed at Oxford: Horace Hart, Printer to the University. Dedicated "To Dr Moritz Steinschneider, the nestor of Jewish bibliography, in commemoration of his eightieth birthday".

REVIEW

Lévi, I. Revue bibliographique. (*R.E.J.* tom. 36, 1898, pp. 115–116.)

89. Talmudical fragments in the Bodleian Library: (1) Fragment of the Talmud Babli, Tractate Kerithoth of the year 1123, the oldest dated MS. of this Talmud. (2) Fragment of the Talmud Jerushalmi, Tractate Berachoth. Edited, with introduction, by S. Schechter, M.A., Reader in Talmudic in the University of Cambridge, and the Rev. S. Singer. *Cambridge: at the University Press,* 1896. 2 p. l., (1)4–6, 28 pp., 2 l., 1 facs. F°.

Hebrew title-page reads:

קונטרסים מתלמוד בבלי כריתות ותלמוד ירושלמי ברכות
מכתבי יד היותר עתיקים בעולם אשר נמצאו בגניזה בארץ מצרים
והנם כעת בבית אוצר הספרים באקספרד. הוצאו לאור ע"י הצעיר
שניאור זלמן שעכטער... והצעיר שמעון סינגער...

Oxford MSS. Heb. b. 1 and D. 45 (Neubauer-Cowley Catalogue, cols. 75–77, nos. 2673–2674). Dedicated to I. H. Weiss, on the occasion of his eightieth birthday "as a token of their admiration for what he has achieved in kindred fields and of personal gratitude for what they owe to him". See *Am. Heb.* vol. 58, 1895–96, p. 726 (announcement of publication).

REVIEW

BACHER, W. Talmudical fragments. (*J.Q.R.* vol. 9, 1897, pp. 145–151.)

90. A fragment of the original text of Ecclesiasticus. (*Expositor.* London, 1896. Ser. 5, vol. 4, pp. 1–15.)

Discovered in the Lewis-Gibson Collection [now in Westminster College] on May 13, 1896. The first information of the acquisition and the identification of the leaf was given by Mrs Lewis in *Academy*, May 16, 1896, in *British Weekly*, by Mrs Gibson, and by E. Nestle in *Allgemeine Zeitung, Beilage*, no. 116, May 20, 1896.

90*a*. —— (*J.C.* July 3, 1896, p. 6.)

Hebrew text and English translation, preceded by comments [by I. Abrahams ?]. See also pp. 14–15 (comments), and Sept. 4, p. 17.

REVIEWS

A[BRAHAMS], I. A fragment of the Hebrew original of Ecclesiasticus discovered by S. Schechter. (*J.C.* May 22, 1896, p. 15.)
See also pp. 13–14.

BACHER, W. [Review.] (*J.Q.R.* vol. 9, pp. 543–562.)

BUDDE, K. [Review.] (*Deutsche, Das, Wochenblatt,* 1896.)

MARGOLIOUTH, D. S. Observations on the fragment of Ecclesiasticus edited by Mr Schechter. (*Expositor.* London, 1896. Ser. 5, vol. 4, pp. 140–151.)

NESTLE, E. [Review.] (*Theologische Literaturzeitung*, Jahrg. 21, 1896, no. 16, cols. 418–419.)

WILSON, R. D. Hebrew fragment of Ecclesiasticus. (*Presbyterian and Reformed Review*, vol. 11, pp. 480 ff.)

91. Some aspects of rabbinic theology: The "Law". (*J.Q.R.* vol. 8, 1896, pp. 1–16.)

Corresponds, in book, with chaps. VIII (The "Law") and IX (The Law as personified in the literature).

92. BUBER, SALOMON. Midrasch Suta.... *Berlin*, 1894. 8°. [Review of.] (*J.Q.R.* vol. 8, 1896, pp. 179–184.)

Differs but slightly from the German (no. 86). Buber's edition contains also the *Agadat Shir ha-Shirim*.

93. Some aspects of rabbinic theology. VI. The Torah in its aspect of law. (*J.Q.R.* vol. 8, 1896, pp. 363–380.)

Corresponds, in book, with chaps. X (The Torah in its aspect of law: Mizwoth) and XI (The joy of the Law). The several instalments are numbered as follows: first instalment: I and II; second instalment: II (should read III); third instalment: III (should read IV); fourth instalment: The "Law" (not numbered); fifth instalment: VI.

1897

94. Notes on a Hebrew commentary to the Pentateuch in a Parma manuscript. (*In* Semitic studies in memory of Alexander Kohut. *Berlin*, 1897. Pp. 485–494. 8°.)

Codex De Rossi 541. Short description of, and extracts from, the first 107 folios. According to S., the commentary originated in the schools of the Tosafists of the thirteenth century, and the compiler was Nathanael the pupil of Jehiel of Paris. The commentary is mentioned by Zunz (Z. *Gesch. u. Lit.* pp. 74, 83) by the title of נימוקי חומש, and noted in Benjacob (p. 398, no. 183).

REVIEW

BACHER, W. Bibliographie. (*R.E.J.* tom. 35, 1897, p. 128.)

95. Facts and fictions about Aquila. (By an occasional correspondent.) (*J.C.* Oct. 15, 1897, p. 21.)

Anonymous. See 102*a* (note).

96. The Lewis-Gibson Hebrew collection. (*J.Q.R.* vol. 9, 1897, pp. 115–121.)

Short list of its treasures. Reads: "To be continued"; but no more published.

97. [Letter to the editor; announcing the discovery of further fragments of the original Ecclesiasticus.] (*Times* [London], July 5, 1897.)

98. A hoard of Hebrew manuscripts. (*Times* [London], Aug. 3, 1897.)

About the Cairo Genizah, its extent and significance; written shortly after his return from Egypt. Extract in *J.C.* Aug. 6, 1897, p. 16. See also p. 19 (comment by an anonymous writer). See also July 9, p. 20 (comment by I. Abrahams).

98 a. —— (*Revue archéologique.* Paris, 1897. Sér. 3, vol. 31, pp. 291–296.) [From the *Times.*]

98 b. A hunt in the Genizah. (*Sunday-school Times* [Philadelphia], vol. 39, 1897, pp. 467 ff.)

98 c. —— (*Jewish Messenger* [New York], Aug. 6, 1897, pp. 1–2.) [From *Sunday-school Times.*]

98 d. —— (*Reform Advocate.* Chicago, 1897–98. Vol. 14, pp. 441–443.) [From *Sunday-school Times.*]

98 e. A hoard of Hebrew manuscripts. I. (*In his* Studies in Judaism, ser. 2, pp. 1–11.)

98 f. Ein Schatz von hebräischen Handschriften. (*Allgemeine Zeitung des Judenthums.* Berlin, 1897. Jahrg. 61, pp. 510–513.)

99. A hoard of MSS. (*Times* [London], Aug. 8, 1897.)

Letter to the editor; reply to an anonymous correspondent, according to whom S. "omits to mention that the discovery of this treasure belongs truly to... Dr A. Neubauer.... The other who went to that 'hiding place'... was Mr Elkan N. Adler, who... practically gave the key to it to Mr Schechter." The letter of the anonymous correspondent is reprinted in *Revue archéologique*, sér. 3, vol. 31, 1897, p. 297.

1898

100. Testimonial. (*In* Abrahams, Israel. Testimonials: Israel Abrahams, M.A. [*London*, 1898.] P. 13.)

101. The Hebrew Ecclesiasticus. (*Expository Times.* Edinburgh, 1898–99. Vol. 10, pp. 567–568.)

102. Work in the Cambridge-Cairo Genizah. (*J.C.* April 1, 1898, pp. 26–27.)

With illustration: "Mr Schechter at work on MSS. from the Cairo Genizah."

102 a. A hoard of Hebrew manuscripts. II. (*In his* Studies in Judaism, ser. 2, pp. 12–30.)

The story of Aquila and his work, dwelled upon here, is reprinted, with the omission of a few paragraphs, from no. 95. See also *J.C.* March 17, 1899, p. 25 ("More Aquila"; concerning further finds).

103. The Cambridge Hebrew Congregation. Celebration of tenth anniversary. (By a graduate.) (*J.C.* Dec. 9, 1898, p. 10.)

Toast to S., and his reply.

104. The rabbinical conception of holiness. (*J.Q.R.* vol. 10, 1898, pp. 1–12.)

Corresponds, in book, with chap. XIII (The law of holiness and the law of goodness). See *J.C.* Oct. 29, 1897, p. 27 (notice).

105. Genizah specimens: Ecclesiasticus [xlix. 12–l. 22]. (*J.Q.R.* vol. 10, 1898, pp. 197–206.)

The series of texts under the title of 'Genizah Specimens' "will...enable the student to form some idea of the nature of this strange literary deposit". This text "represents a specimen of the new discoveries of the original Hebrew of Ecclesiasticus made by me during the summer months of 1897". See *J.C.* July 9, 1897, p. 14 ("Mr Schechter's latest treasure trove"; editorial comment); Oct. 8, p. 23; Jan. 21, 1898, p. 27.

—— Lévi, I. Notes exégétiques sur un nouveau fragment de l'original hébreu de l'Ecclésiastique. (*R.E.J.* tom. 37, 1898, pp. 210–217.)

106. Genizah specimens: Liturgy. (*J.Q.R.* vol. 10, 1898, pp. 654–659.)

The fragments, "all written in very ancient hands, represent as it seems portions of the liturgy in their oldest form". The Palestinian version of *Shemoneh Esreh* was reprinted, with vowel-points, by G. Dalman, *Die Worte Jesu* (Leipzig, 1898, Bd. 1; also in his "Sonderabdruck", *Messianische Texte*, 1898); and in H. L. Strack's edition of *Mischna Berakoth* (Leipzig, 1915).

1899

107. The Wisdom of Ben Sira. Portions of the book Ecclesiasticus [3–7, 11–16, 30–33, 35–38, 49–51] from Hebrew manuscripts in the Cairo Genizah collection presented to the University of Cambridge by the editors. Edited for the Syndics of the University Press by S. Schechter, M.A., Litt.D., Reader in Rabbinic in the University of Cambridge and Professor of Hebrew in the University of London, and C. Taylor, D.D., Master of St John's College, Cambridge. *Cambridge: at the University Press*, 1899. lxxxvii, 68, 24 pp., 2 facs. Sq. 4°.

Hebrew title: ‏חכמת שמעון בן ישוע בן אלעזר בן סירא.

Contents: [Preface by C. T.] I. The translation: Portions of Ecclesiasticus 3–16 and 30–51 [rather, 3–7, 11–16, 30–33, 35–38, 49–51] translated [by C. T.] from Cairo Genizah Hebrew manuscripts with footnotes. II. Appendix: Notes on the Lewis-Gibson and Oxford folios [by C. T.]; the alphabetic poem in Ecclesiasticus 51 [by C. T.]; facsimiles of the Lewis-Gibson folio. III. The text [22 pp.; 20 of which edited by S. for the first time; pp. 21–22 (chap. 49.12–50.22) previously published by S. (no. 105)]; prefatory note [by S.]; introduction [by S.]; notes on the text [by S.].

REVIEWS

ABRAHAMS, I. The Wisdom of Ben Sira. (*J.C.* July 21, 1899, p. 22.)
See also July 14, p. 30 (announcement of publication).
—— The Wisdom of Ben Sira. (Preliminary notice.) (*J.Q.R.* vol. 12, 1900, pp. 171–176.)
BEVAN, A. A. The Wisdom of Ben Sira. (*Journal of Theological Studies*, vol. 1, 1900, pp. 135–143.)
JACOBS, J. A romance in scholarship. (*Fortnightly Review*, vol. 72, pp. 696–704.)
—— —— (*Living Age*, vol. 223, pp. 762 ff.)
—— —— (*Eclectic Magazine*, vol. 134, pp. 158 ff.)
NOELDEKE, T. Bemerkungen zum hebräischen Ben Sira. (*Z.A.W.* vol. 20, 1900, pp. 81–94.)
See also *J.C.* Feb. 16, 1900, p. 24 (reference).
SMEND, R. [Review.] (*Theologische Literaturzeitung*, Jahrg. 24, 1899, cols. 505–509.)
See also *J.C.* Sept. 8, 1899, p. 19 (reference). For further literature, see Seydl, E., Bericht über die Sirach-Literatur, 1897–1900, *Wien: Selbstverlag des Verfassers*, 1901. [Reprinted from Literarischer Anzeiger für das Kath. Oesterreich.] Peters, N., Litteraturverzeichnis. (*In his* Der jüngst wiederaufgefundene hebräische Text des Buches Ecclesiasticus..., *Freiburg i. Br.* 1902, pp. vii–xi.) Peters, N., Conspectus editionum textus adhibitarum. Alii libri maioris momenti. (*In his edition* Liber Iesu filii Sirach sive Ecclesiasticus Hebraice..., *Freiburg i. Br.* 1905, pp. xi–xiv.) Peters, N., Literaturverzeichnis. (*In his* Das Buch Jesus Sirach oder Ecclesiasticus..., *Münster i. W.* 1913, pp. xi–xv.)

108. MARGOLIOUTH, DAVID SAMUEL. The origin of the "original Hebrew" of Ecclesiasticus. *London*, 1899. 4°. [Criticism of.] (*Critical Review of Theological and Philosophical Literature*. Edinburgh, 1899. Vol. 9, pp. 387–400; vol. 10, 1900, pp. 116–129.)

M. reviews the Cowley-Neubauer edition of the Oxford fragments; maintains that the Ben Sira is a retranslation. See *J.C.* June 16, 1899, p. 26 ("Professor D. S. Margoliouth on Ecclesiasticus") and June 23, p. 24 ("Professor D. S. Margoliouth on Ecclesiasticus XLIII, 17 c").

109. The Hebrew Ecclesiasticus. (*Expository Times*, vol. 10, 1898–99, pp. 568.)

A reply to D. S. Margoliouth's article under the same heading in *Expository Times*, vol. 10, p. 528.

110. Professor Schechter's introductory lecture [of a course of lectures on the Hebrew text of Ecclesiasticus] at University College, [London, Jan. 26, 1899]. (*J.C.* Feb. 3, 1899, p. 10.)

Report of inaugural lecture; against the "Higher criticism" of the radical school. See also Feb. 17, p. 23, and April 14, p. 26.

110*a*. The study of the Bible. (*In his* Studies in Judaism, ser. 2, pp. 31–54; notes, pp. 309–310.)

111. [Response to the addresses made at the dinner given by the London Maccabaeans on the occasion of his appointment as Professor of Hebrew at the University College, London.] (*J.C.* Feb. 3, 1899, p. 14.)

See also p. 18.

112. In memoriam of Mrs N. S. Joseph. (*J.C.* March 24, 1899, p. 11.)

113. Geniza specimens: A letter of Chushiel. [With facsimile.] (*J.Q.R.* vol. 11, 1899, pp. 643–650.)

Chushiel (or Hushiel) ben Elhanan was president of the Bet ha-Midrash at Kairwan toward the end of the tenth century. The letter, addressed to Shemariah ben Elhanan, chief rabbi of Cairo, shows that both emigrated from Italy, and thus discredits the story of the "four captives" (i.e. Hushiel, Moses ben Enoch, Shemariah, and an unknown) made by the Arab admiral Ibn Rumahis, as related by Abraham Ibn Daud in his *Sefer ha-Kabbalah*, with whom Jewish history in the West was supposed to have had its beginning. See *J.C.* April 1, 1898, p. 17 ("A historic letter of Rabbi Chushiel", by N. R.). See also July 14, 1899, p. 30 and July 21, p. 23 (references).

1900

114. נוסחא בקדיש. מאת ד' שעכטער (*In* Gedenkbuch zur Erinnerung an David Kaufmann. *Breslau*, 1900. [Heb. sec.], pp. 52–54. 8°.)

Paged also i–iii. Genizah fragment of the Kaddish, remarkable, among other things, for the honorific insertion, during their lifetime, of the names of the three heads of the Jews in Egypt in the latter half of the eleventh century.

114a. —— No t.-p. [*Breslau*, 1900.] 3 pp. 8°.

115. Is the external evidence really against the Cairene Ecclesiasticus? (*Expository Times*, vol. 11, 1899–1900, pp. 140–142.)

A reply to the arguments of D. S. Margoliouth in *Expository Times*, vol. 11, pp. 90–92.

116. The Hebrew Sirach. (*Expository Times*, vol. 11, 1899–1900, pp. 285–287.)

Against D. S. Margoliouth's arguments in *Expository Times*, vol. 11, pp. 191–192.

3-2

117. The Hebrew Sirach. (*Expository Times*, vol. 11, 1899–1900, pp. 382–383.)

Further evidence of its "originality".

118. The Hebrew Sirach. (*Expository Times*, vol. 11, 1899–1900, pp. 522–523.)

Additional proofs.

119. Professor Schechter at University College, [London]. (*J.C.* Jan. 26, 1900, p. 25.)

Report of a public lecture on the social life of Judaea in the time of Sirach, Jan. 18, 1900.

120. Dinner to Mr Joseph Jacobs. (*J.C.* Feb. 23, 1900, pp. 18–19.)

Toast by S. who presided.

121. The late Rev. L. M. Simmons: In memoriam. (*J.C.* April 13, 1900, p. 12.)

122. The MSS. from the Cairo Geniza. Report of the Reader in Talmudic on the Taylor-Schechter collection. (*J.C.* June 22, 1900, p. 25.)

Reprinted from Cambridge University Library, Annual report of the Library Syndicate, no. 47.

123. Professor Schechter at University College, [London]. (*J.C.* June 29, 1900, p. 28.)

Report of a public lecture on the state of Judaea in the time of Sirach, June 21, 1900.

124. Jews and Anglo-Saxons. (*J.C.* Oct. 12, 1900, p. 6.)

Epistle 1 of the *Four epistles to the Jews of England*, in criticism of certain theological catchwords then current. This epistle provoked a great deal of controversy. See *J.C.* Oct. 19, 1900, pp. 6–7; Oct. 26, pp. 7–8; Nov. 2, pp. 6–8; Nov. 9, pp. 6–8, 17; Nov. 16, pp. 8–10, 18; Nov. 23, pp. 8–9.

125. Jews as missionaries. (*J.C.* Oct. 26, 1900, p. 7.)
Epistle 2.

126. Spiritual religion *v.* spiritual men. (*J.C.* Nov. 30, 1900, p. 9.)
Epistle 3. See also pp. 16–17.

127. Genizah specimens. (*J.Q.R.* vol. 12, 1900, pp. 112–113.)

..."probably written somewhere in Spain in the eleventh century, and seem to represent a letter of introduction given to a person emigrating to Egypt....The cause of the emigration seems to have been some general persecution....Perhaps we have here a reference to the troubles which followed the assassination of Joseph ibn Nagdila in...1066." The signatories to the letter are: Samuel b. Isaac, Isaac b. Joseph, and Samuel b. Judah, "who seem to represent the Beth Din of a Spanish community". See *J.C.* Nov. 3, p. 25 (reference).

128. The Hebrew text of Ben Sira: The British Museum fragments of Ecclesiasticus. (*J.Q.R.* vol. 12, 1900, pp. 266–272.)

Offers "some alternative emendations or differing explanations of the text" of the British Museum fragments edited by G. Margoliouth (*J.Q.R.* vol. 12, pp. 1–33). S., by the way, defends also his thesis of the Paitanic tendency of Ben Sira, pointing out "that the Paitan is by no means a post-Talmudic product".

—— MARGOLIOUTH, G. Ben-Sira and the Paitanim. (*J.C.* Feb. 2, 1900, p. 9.)

—— CHOTZNER, J. Ben-Sira and the Paitanim. (*J.C.* Feb. 9, 1900, p. 7.)

See *J.C.* Sept. 23, 1892, p. 13 (note on S.'s earlier suggestions concerning the *Piyutim.* See also *J.C.* Feb. 13, 1903, pp. 26–27, "Ben Sira as a source of hymnology").

129. Some rabbinic parallels to the New Testament. (*J.Q.R.* vol. 12, 1900, pp. 415–433.)

Paper read before the Hebrew class at University College, London, Oct. 19, 1899. Condensed report in *J.C.* Oct. 27, 1899, p. 19 and May 4, 1900, p. 23.

129*a*. On the study of the Talmud. (*In his* Studies in Judaism, ser. 2, pp. 102–125; notes, pp. 311–313.)

130. A further fragment of Ben-Sira. (*J.Q.R.* vol. 12, 1900, pp. 456–465.)

Discovered in the Cairo Collection of Cambridge University Library, called MS. C; 2 leaves; paper. The contents of three other Genizah fragments "having some bearing upon the Ben Sira question" are also reproduced: (1) 2 leaves; paper; "represents a collection of proverbs and sayings". (2) 2 leaves; paper; "containing jottings from...Bible and Talmud, and its commentaries (Arabic)". (3) Scrap of paper, Arabic, in Hebrew letters, which "must come from a MS. containing a commentary to the T. B. Sanhedrin"; copy and translation "prepared for me by Mr H. Pass and the Rev. Dr Arendzen". See *J.C.* Feb. 16, 1900, p. 9 (notice). See also Taylor, C., "The Wisdom of Ben Sira" (*Journal of Theological Studies*, vol. 1, 1900; especially pp. 575–578). See also *ib.* p. 473 (notice by W. E. B[arnes]).

1901

131. The Jewish Encyclopedia.... *New York*, 1901–5. 12 vols. 4°.

S. was a member of the Foreign Board of Consulting Editors: 1901–2 (for vols. 1–2); member of the American Board of Consulting Editors: 1903–5 (for vols. 3–12); member of Editorial Board (editorial supervision of the Talmudic department) for vols. 4–7. Vols. 4–10 lists S. among the contributors; but I found no articles signed by him. See *J. Comment*, vol. 20, no. 5, p. 9 (article by A. M. F[riedenberg]).

132. Despising a glorious inheritance. (*J.C.* Feb. 15, 1901, pp. 9–10.)
Epistle 4.

132 *a.* Four epistles to the Jews of England. By Professor S. Schechter, Litt.D., M.A. (of Cambridge).... *London: "Jewish Chronicle" Office*, 1901. 15 pp. 8°.

132 *b.* —— (*In his* Studies in Judaism, ser. 2, pp. 182–201.)

133. The ideal of a Jewish theological seminary. (*J.C.* April 26, 1901, pp. 12–14.)
With portrait. Address at the prize distribution at Jews' College, London, April 21, 1901; subheaded: Soul-wisdom cannot be pigeon-holed or labelled; Wisdom a combination of reason and emotion; Lifelong teachers must be lifelong learners; The true purpose of Jews' College; Discovery of an ancient MS. an act of resurrection; Lifelong devotion to study. See *J.C.* May 30, 1913, p. 29 (reference).

133 *a.* —— (*In* Jews' College. Jubilee volume. *London*, 1906. Pp. cxlvi–clii. 8°.)

134. Lector M. Friedmann: Celebration of his seventieth birthday. (*J.C.* June 28, 1901, p. 17.)

135. Geniza specimens: A marriage settlement. (*J.Q.R.* vol. 13, 1901, pp. 218–221.)
MS. T-S. 241; Ketubah, dated 1082, "between the Rabbanite bridegroom David Hannasi the son of Daniel Hannasi, and the Karaite bride Nasia the daughter of R. Moses, the son of Aaron the priest".

136. Geniza specimens: The oldest collection of Bible difficulties, by a Jew. (*J.Q.R.* vol. 13, 1901, pp. 345–374.)

MS. T-S. 6*; 6 leaves. See Davidson, I., *Saadia's polemic
against Hiwi Al-Balkhi* (New York, 1915), p. 19, footnote:
"I may add, that long before our text came to light, I had the
privilege of learning from him [S.] by word of mouth that he no
longer regarded that hypothesis [i.e. that these *Genizah specimens*
are identical with Hiwi Al-Balkhi's *Two hundred questions*]
as tenable."

REVIEWS

BACHER, W. Zu Schechter's neuestem Geniza-Funde.
(*J.Q.R.* vol. 13, 1901, pp. 741–745.)

GOTTHEIL, R. J. H. Some early Jewish Bible criticism.
(*Journal of Biblical Literature*, vol. 23, 1904, pp. 1–12 [es-
pecially pp. 8–12].)

KAHANA, D. שאלות עתיקות. (הגרן. [Berditchev, 1906.]
Vol. 5, pp. 5–42.)
With text.

PORGES, N. Zu Schechter's neuestem Geniza-Funde.
(*J.Q.R.* vol. 14, 1902, pp. 129–133.)

—— Eine Geniza-Studie. (*J.Q.R.* vol. 20, 1908, pp. 187–
210.)

POZNANSKI, S. Einige vorläufige Bemerkungen zu dem
Geniza-Fragment.... (*J.Q.R.* vol. 13, 1901, pp. 746–749.)

SELIGSOHN, M. Une critique de la Bible du temps des
Gueonim. (*R.E.J.* tom. 46, 1903, pp. 99–122.)
With translation of document. See also *J.C.* May 3, 1901,
p. 27.

1902

137. Midrash Hag-gadol; forming a collection of
ancient rabbinic homilies to the Pentateuch.
Edited for the first time from various Yemen
manuscripts, and provided with notes and
preface by S. Schechter, M.A., Litt.D., Reader
in Rabbinic in the University of Cambridge,
Professor of Hebrew in University College,
London. [Vol. 1] Genesis. *Cambridge: at the
University Press*, 1902. xxviii pp., 772 cols.
[= 386 pp.], 773–825(1) pp. Sq. 4°.

BIBLIOGRAPHY

Hebrew title-page reads:

מדרש הגדול על חמשה חומשי תורה. ספר בראשית. הוציא
לאור על פי כת״י מארץ תימן עם הערות והקדמה שניאור זלמן
שעכטער... קנטאבריגיא, תרסב.

The text printed at Vienna by M. Knöpflmacher. "Dedicated to the memory of Dr Asher Asher and his wife, Mrs Lucy Asher."

This "homiletic Thesaurus" was compiled by a Yemenite Jew of the fourteenth century. As the basis of this edition, S. used a MS. presented to him by C. G. Montefiore, and one of G. A. Kohut, "the oldest and most accurate of all MSS.", but not known to the editor until the work was nearly ready for the press [see end of note]. "My work as editor has consisted chiefly in arranging the text after the chapters and verses of the section in the Scriptures which the various homilies are meant to illustrate; in separating texts from commentaries by brief indications in the notes, and tracing the sources of our author through the literature of the ancient Rabbis and their successors. Where these traces were lost in the extant works I have drawn special attention to the fact, or suggested the name of the writing where the passage in question may have occurred." The first reference to this work of S. is found in an article by A. Neubauer, "Progress of Midraschic literature" (*J.C.* Sept. 25, 1885, p. 12), where he says: "I believe that Mr Schechter, after having finished his splendid and very critical edition of the *Aboth de R. Nathan*, will devote his great knowledge of the Halakhic and Aggadic literature to an edition of the great Midrash." S., himself, refers to his work on the "Great Midrash" in 1890 (see no. 41, note). For other references, see *J.C.* Dec. 30, 1892, p. 15; June 22, 1894, p. 17; May 19, 1899, p. 20. See also Kohut, G. A., "A memoir of Dr Alexander Kohut's Literary activity", in *Tributes to the memory of Rev. Dr Alexander Kohut* (New York, 1894), p. 63, where it is stated that A. Kohut "had hoped...together with Mr Schechter, in Cambridge, to publish the newly found Yemen Midrash Ha-Gadol".

REVIEWS

A[BRAHAMS], I. Professor Schechter's edition of the Midrash Hag-gadol. (*J.C.* Sept. 12, 1902, p. 18.)

COWLEY, A. E. [Review.] (*Journal of Theological Studies*, vol. 4, 1903, pp. 624–625.)

41

GINZBERG, L. Professor Schechter's new book. (*J. Comment*, vol. 16, 1902–3, no. 14, pp. 1–2.)

LÉVI, I. Bibliographie. (*R.E.J.* tom. 46, 1903, pp. 277–278.)

138. Report of the Curator of Oriental Literature on the Taylor-Schechter Collection. (*In* Cambridge University Library. Report of the Library Syndicate for the year ending Dec. 31, 1901. Cambridge, 1902. P. 7.)

From the University Reporter, 1901–2.

139. The emancipation of Jewish science. (*Am. Heb.* vol. 71, 1902, pp. 69–70.)

Address delivered at the Judaean banquet, May 29, 1902. See also pp. 75–76. Also *J. Comment*, vol. 15, 1902, no. 8, p. 14.

139 *a*. —— (*In his* Seminary addresses and other papers, pp. 1–7.)

140. The meaning and scope of the Jewish Theological Seminary. (*Am. Heb.* vol. 72, 1902–3, pp. 67–71.)

See also p. 36 (editorial comment), and pp. 37–38 (report).

140 *a*. The inaugural address of Professor Solomon Schechter. (*J. Comment*, vol. 16, 1902–3, no. 7, pp. 1–6.)

With portrait. See also p. 8 (editorial comment), and no. 6, p. 11 (report). Also *J.C.* Dec. 19, 1902, p. 18.

140 *b*. Inaugural address as President of the Faculty of the Jewish Theological Seminary of America, delivered November 20, 1902. *New York*, 1903. 35 pp. 8°.

140*c*. The inaugural address of Professor Solomon Schechter. (*In* Jewish Theological Seminary of America. Biennial report, 1902–4. *New York*, 1906. Pp. 84–101. 8°.)

140*d*. The charter of the Seminary. (*In his* Seminary addresses and other papers, pp. 9–33.)

141. [The universality of Judaism.] (*J.C.* March 14, 1902, p. 14.)

Condensed report of an informal address at the inauguration of the Schechter Society at Cambridge University.

142. Presentation to Dr Schechter [of an engrossed testimonial and a clock from Scholars and Professors of Cambridge University]. (*J.C.* March 14, 1902, p. 13.)

A response to addresses of John Peile and Charles Taylor at presentation in Combination Room of Christ's College. See also March 21, p. 10 ("The Schechter testimonial").

143. Farewell dinner to Prof. and Mrs Schechter. (*J.C.* April 11, 1902, pp. 13–14.)

With portrait. Held at the Trocadero Restaurant, London, April 6; principal toasts by Chief Rabbi H. Adler and I. Zangwill; response by S. See also p. 19 ("The Schechter banquet"; editorial comment). Also *J. Comment*, vol. 15, 1902, no. 2, p. 8 (report).

144. [The uses of Hebrew manuscripts.] (*J. Comment*, vol. 15, 1902, no. 14, p. 7.)

Report of a lecture before the Jewish Chautauqua Assembly.

145. Dr Schechter talks about the Seminary. (*J. Comment*, vol. 15, 1902, no. 24, p. 5.)

Interview with A. M. Friedenberg.

146. Reception to Dr Schechter by the Ohole Shem
Society [of New York]. (*J. Comment*, vol. 16,
1902–3, no. 2, p. 6.)

S. spoke in German; only gist of remarks reported by A. M.
Friedenberg.

147. Geniza specimens: Saadyana. Articles 1–3.
[With 3 facs.] (*J.Q.R.* vol. 14, 1902, pp.
37–63, 197–249, 449–516.)

Articles 2 and 3 bear the title "Saadyana".

REVIEWS

BACHER, W. Die von Schechter edirten Saadyana. (*J.Q.R.*
vol. 14, 1902, pp. 740–741.)

—— Aus einer alten Poetik (Schule Saadja's). [German
translation of Arabic fragment no. LI; with comments.]
(*J.Q.R.* vol. 14, 1902, pp. 742–744.)

—— Ein neuerschlossenes Capitel der jüdischen Geschichte.
[Pertaining to fragment no. XL (new no. XXXVIII).]
(*J.Q.R.* vol. 15, 1903, pp. 79–96.)

GOLDZIHER, I. Zu Saadyana XLI [new no. XL]. (*J.Q.R.*
vol. 15, 1903, pp. 73–75.)

See also *Theologischer Jahresbericht*, Bd. 22, 1902, p. 283.

148. Saadyana. Geniza fragments of writings of R.
Saadya Gaon and Others. Edited by S.
Schechter, M.A., Litt.D. (Cantab.), President
of the Faculty of the Jewish Theological
Seminary of America. *Cambridge: Deighton
& Bell*, 1903. xii, 148 pp. 8°.

Dedication: "To my master, Lector M. Friedmann of
Vienna, this volume is dedicated in gratitude and admiration."
The edition is enlarged by a Preface, Corrections and additions,
and by the Fragment IV *b*. The facsimiles are omitted, and the
arrangement differs somewhat from that in the *J.Q.R.* "The
fragments...belong with few exceptions to the Taylor-
Schechter Collection of the University Library at Cambridge,
England. The exceptions are fragments VII [formerly in

possession of M. Sulzberger; now J.T.S.A.], XLIII, XLVIII
[Collection E. N. Adler; now J.T.S.A.]....The various fragments...are provided with short introductions describing the
MSS. and indicating the nature of their varying contents."
They are published in the order of their discovery. Most of the
fragments "either date from the Gaon himself or have at least
a bearing upon his life and works".

REVIEWS

Poznanski, S. Schechter's Saadyana. (*Zeitschrift für hebraeische Bibliographie*, Jahrg. 7, 1903, pp. 107–113, 142–147,
178–187.)
Anhang I: Alphabetischer Index der Personennamen.
Anhang II: Bücherverzeichnisse; 1. Ein Sammelband aus dem
Jahre 1174; 2. Fragment einer Bücherliste; 3. Ein Biblio-
theksverzeichnis.

———— *Frankfurt-a.-M.: J. Kauffmann*, 1904, 23 pp. 8°.
See also Poznanski, S., "Ephraim ben Schemaria de Fostat
et l'académie palestinienne" (*R.E.J.* tom. 48, 1904, pp. 145–
171 [reference to Saadyana, pp. 160ff.]); and his "Zur Geschichte der palästinensischen Geonim, 943–1138" (*Z.D.M.G.*
Bd. 68, 1914, pp. 118–128). See also Marmorstein, A., "Über
das Geonat in Palästina, 980–1160 n. Chr." (*Z.D.M.G.* Bd.
67, 1913, pp. 635–644). Also *J.C.* Jan. 23, 1903, p. 27
(reference).

1903

149. Asher I. Myers. [Obituary]. (*In* American
    Jewish Historical Society. Publications. [*Balti-
    more*], 1903. No. 11, pp. 204–206. 8°.)

150. Genizah MS. (*In* Festschrift zum siebzigsten
    Geburtstage A. Berliner's. *Frankfurt.-a.-M.*,
    1903. [Heb. sec.], pp. 108–112. 8°.)

Represents letter and postscript in Hebrew, addressed by
Elijah ha-Kohen ben Abraham at Fostat (before 1038) to
Jacob ben Joseph in Aleppo. The drift of the letter is described
in the English introduction. See *J.C.* June 12, 1903, p. 22
(comment).

45

150*a*. —— *Berlin: H. Itzkowski,* 1903. 5 pp. 8°.

REVIEW

POZNANSKI, S. Bibliographie. (*R.E.J.* tom. 47, 1903, p. 139.)

151. Address [delivered at Judaean banquet in honour of K. Kohler, March 26, 1903]. (*Am. Heb.* vol. 72, 1902–3, pp. 654–655.)

151*a*. —— (*J. Comment,* vol. 16, 1902–3, no. 26, pp. 1–3.)

See also p. 8 (editorial comment).

151*b*. Higher criticism—higher anti-Semitism. (*In his* Seminary addresses and other papers, pp. 35–39.)

152. The mission of the Seminary. (*Am. Heb.* vol. 72, 1902–3, pp. 789–791.)

Address delivered at the dedication of the J.T.S.A. building, April 26, 1903.

152*a*. The Jewish Theological Seminary of America. (*Chicago Israelite,* Dec. 12, 1903.)

152*b*. —— (*J. Comment,* vol. 17, 1903, no. 3, pp. 11–13.)

See also *J.C.* May 15, 1903, p. 29.

152*c*. —— (*Menorah.* New York, 1903. Vol. 34, pp. 297–304.)

152*d*. The mission of the Seminary. (*In* Jewish Theological Seminary of America. Biennial report, 1902–4. *New York,* 1906. Pp. 108–116. 8°.)

152*e*. The Seminary as a witness. (*In his* Seminary addresses and other papers, pp. 41–51.)

153. A man of full stature. [Address at memorial service of Marcus M. Jastrow, Philadelphia, Nov. 5, 1903.] (*Am. Heb.* vol. 73, 1903, pp. 791–793.)

153*a*. Professor Schechter's tribute to Rabbi Marcus M. Jastrow. (*J. Comment*, vol. 18, 1903–4, no. 4, pp. 1–3.)

153*b*. A man of full stature. (*Menorah*. New York, 1903. Vol. 35, pp. 335–341.)

153*c*. —— (*Reform Advocate*. Chicago, 1903–4. Vol. 26, pp. 459–561.)

153*d*. Dr Jastrow's work and influence. Dr Jastrow as a scholar. (*In* Philadelphia, Pa. Congregation Rodeph Shalom. Annual no. 11, 1903–4. *Philadelphia*, 1904. Pp. 35–43.)

154. [The Synagogue.] (*J. Comment*, vol. 18, 1903–4, no. 8, p. 7.)

Lecture at the Mickve Israel Synagogue, Philadelphia, Nov. 29, 1903; partial report headed: Prof. Schechter lectures in Philadelphia.

155. A talk with Dr Schechter. (*J.C.* Aug. 28, 1903, p. 18.)

About American Jewish conditions; interviewed in London. See *Reform Advocate*, vol. 26, p. 88 (editorial comment by E. G. Hirsch). See also *Am. Heb.* vol. 73, 1903, p. 537 (comment).

156. Miszelle. (*Zeitschrift für hebraeische Bibliographie*, Jahrg. 7, 1903, p. 192.)

Pertaining to a fragment published by A. Harkavy (originally in *R.E.J.* tom. 45, 1902, pp. 298–305), which according to S. forms part of a fragment he was about to publish. See no. 165.

1904

157. Talmud. (*In* Dictionary of the Bible...ed. by
    J. Hastings.... *New York*, 1904. Extra
    volume [being vol. 5], pp. 57–66. 4°.)
See *J.C.* Aug. 5, 1904, p. 21 and Sept. 9, p. 18.

157*a*. —— (*In his* Studies in Judaism, ser. 3, pp.
    194–237.)

158. [Testimonial.] (*In* Hertz, Simon, Torath S'fath
    Eber. A Hebrew grammar...in English and
    Jewish-German.... *New York*, 1904. Various
    paging. 8°.)

159. The Seminary and the community. (*Am. Heb.*
    vol. 74, 1903–4, pp. 595–597.)
Address delivered at the biennial meeting of the J.T.S.A.,
March 20, 1904.

159*a*. The work of the Theological Seminary. (*J.
    Comment*, vol. 18, 1903–4, no. 24, pp. 4–7, 9.)

159*b*. The battles of the Torah. (*J. Exponent*, vol. 38,
    1904, no. 23, p. 9.)

159*c*. President Schechter's address. (*In* Jewish
    Theological Seminary of America. Biennial
    report, 1902–4. *New York*, 1906. Pp. 58–66.
    8°.)

159*d*. Spiritual honeymoons. (*In his* Seminary ad-
    dresses and other papers, pp. 53–63.)

160. Professor Schechter's address [at the graduation
    exercises of the Baron de Hirsch Agricultural
    and Industrial School, Woodbine, N.J.]. (*J.
    Comment*, vol. 18, 1903–4, no. 25, pp. 15–16.)

161. In honor of M. Anatole Leroy-Beaulieu. (*Am. Heb.* vol. 75, 1904, pp. 16–21.)
Address delivered at the Judaean banquet.

161*a.* Prof. Schechter's toast. (*J. Comment,* vol. 19, 1904, no. 6, pp. 3–5.)

161*b.* Prof. Schechter's address. (*J. Exponent,* vol. 39, 1904, no. 5, pp. 1–2.)

161*c.* Rebellion against being a problem. (*In* Judaean addresses. *New York,* 1917. Vol. 2, pp. 27–32. 8°.)

162. Professor Schechter and Zionism. (*Am. Heb.* vol. 74, 1903–4, p. 685.)
Statement regarding his reported views.

163. Address [at the graduation exercises of the J.T.S.A., June 5, 1904]. (*Am. Heb.* vol. 75, 1904, pp. 108–109.)

163*a.* ——— (*J. Comment,* vol. 19, 1904, no. 9, pp. 2–5 [and Supplement, p. 1].)

163*b.* The reconciliation of Israel. (*In his* Seminary addresses and other papers, pp. 73–80.)
Last two paragraphs omitted.

164. Altar building in America. (*J. Exponent,* Sept. [?], 1904.)
Address at the consecration of the reconstructed synagogue of Congregation Agudath Jeshurun, Indianapolis, Ind., and the installation of Rabbi Charles I. Hoffman, Aug. 28, 1904. See also *Am. Heb.* vol. 75, 1904, p. 429 (extract).

164*a.* Prof. S. Schechter's address. (*In* Indianapolis, Ind. Congregation Agudath Jeshurun. Dedication and induction at Indianapolis, Ind. [*Indianapolis,* 1904.] 8 pp. 4°.)

164*b*. Altar building in America. (*In his* Seminary addresses and other papers, pp. 81–89.)

165. Genizah fragments. (*J.Q.R.* vol. 16, 1904, pp. 425–452.)
I. Gnomic. II. Halakhic: מכילתא דר׳/ש בן יוחאי. III. מכילתא דברים. I: MS. J.T.S.A. (deposited only ?); 7 leaves; square characters; "by an oriental hand, probably not later than the twelfth century". (See no. 156.) II: MS. Cambridge; 2 leaves; "with a few notes and references to the cognate literature...in places where the text is in rather a corrupt state." Comprises Deuteronomy 11. 31–12. 3, and 12. 27–13. 1. III: MS. Oxford Heb. c. 18; 2 leaves; "representing an ancient Tannaitic Midrash" (Neubauer-Cowley Catalogue, no. 2634: 3, "where it is erroneously described as Sifre"): Deut. 11. 26–29. II and III reprinted in D. Hoffmann's edition of *Midrasch Tannaim*. Dedicated to the memory of David Kaufmann.

165*a*. —— Corrections and additions. (*J.Q.R.* vol. 16, 1904, pp. 776–777.)

REVIEW

Belléli, L. Un nouvel apocryphe. Étude sur un fragment de manuscrit du Vieux Caire. [With reference to I.] *Livorne: S. Belforte et Cie*, 1904, 23 pp. 8°.

See also Levi, B., *Gnomic literature in Bible and Apocrypha* (Chicago, 1917). [Especially note 72, pp. 95–98; also note 27.] Also *J.C.* May 13, 1904, p. 28.

166. The Mechilta to Deuteronomy. (*J.Q.R.* vol. 16, 1904, pp. 695–701.)
MS. T-S. 16. 88; 2 leaves. Deut. 13. 14–19. Reprinted in D. Hoffmann's *Midrasch Tannaim*.

167. Jastrow, Marcus M. A dictionary of the Targumim, the Talmud Babli and Yerushalmi, and the Midraschic literature. *London and New York*, 1903. 4°. [Review of.] (*Times* [New York] *Saturday Review of Books*, Feb. [?], 1904.)

167*a*. The Talmud. (*Menorah.* New York, 1904. Vol. 36, pp. 168–173.)

167*b*. A review of Dr Jastrow's Dictionary of the Talmud. (*Reform Advocate.* Chicago, 1903–4. Vol. 22, pp. 595–597.)

1905

168. A truer Judaism. (*Am. Heb.* vol. 77, 1905, pp. 95–96.)
Address at the graduating exercises of the J.T.S.A., June 18, 1905.

—— DE HAAS, J. A question for Prof. Schechter [relative to his address]. (*Am. Heb.* vol. 77, 1905, p. 128.)

169. Professor Schechter at Cambridge [Mass. Short report of course of lectures on "Early rabbinic theology" at Summer School of Theology of Harvard University Divinity School, July 11–15, 1905.] (*Am. Heb.* vol. 77, 1905, p. 217.)
See also vol. 76, p. 512 (announcement); and *J.C.* May 19, 1905, p. 19.

170. The future of Judaism in the U.S. (*Am. Heb.* vol. 77, pp. 747–748.)
With portrait. Interview.

171. Synod or no synod: Views of President Schechter. (*American Israelite.* Cincinnati, 1904–5. Vol. 51, no. 42, pp. 4–5.)
A communication, dated April 5, 1905, on the advisability of forming a synod of rabbis and laymen; S. opposed its formation. See *J.C.* May 19, 1905, p. 19; June 23, p. 21; also Feb. 14, 1908, pp. 16–17 (article by F. S. Spiers).

171*a.* An American Jewish Synod: The opinion of Dr Schechter. (*Am. Heb.* vol. 76, 1904–5, pp. 697–699.)

See also p. 694 (editorial comment).

171*b.* Views of President Schechter. (*In* Central Conference of American Rabbis. Views on the Synod.... *Baltimore*, 1905. Pp. 134–141. 8°.)

172. The destruction of the original of Ecclesiasticus. (*Expository Times*, vol. 16, 1904–5, pp. 185–186.)

Against D. S. Margoliouth in *Expository Times*, vol. 16, pp. 26–29; גנז means to hide, not to destroy.

173. [Address delivered before the Baltimore Branch of the J.T.S.A., Feb. 15, 1905.] (*J. Comment*, vol. 20, 1904–5, no. 16, p. 16.)

Only one paragraph quoted.

174. Professor Schechter on Jewish saints. (*J. Comment*, vol. 20, 1904–5, no. 19, pp. 2–3.)

The ideals of saints and saintliness as exemplified in Jewish life and literature. Report of lecture delivered at the Congregation B'nai Jeshurun, New York, Feb. 9, 1905, in the course of public lectures of the J.T.S.A. See also *Am. Heb.* vol. 76, 1904–5, pp. 398, 431–432 (reports).

174*a.* Saints and saintliness. (*In his* Studies in Judaism, ser. 2, pp. 148–181; notes, pp. 314–317.)

1906

175. Address at the graduation exercises of the Jewish Theological Seminary, June 10, 1906. (*Am. Heb.* vol. 79, 1906, pp. 29–32.)

With portrait. See also p. 27 (editorial comment).

175*a*. —— (*J. Comment*, vol. 23, 1906, no. 10, pp. 10–13.)

175*b*. —— (*In* Jewish Theological Seminary of America. Biennial report, 1905–6. *New York*, 1906. Pp. 126–128. 8°.)

176. Letter [of congratulation to Chief Rabbi H. Adler on the occasion of the celebration of the Jews' College jubilee]. (*Am. Heb.* vol. 79, 1906, p. 92.)

176*a*. —— (*In* Jews' College, London, Eng. Jubilee volume.... *London*, 1906. Pp. 260–261. 8°.)

177. Address [at the opening session of the J.T.S.A., Oct. 22, 1906]. (*Am. Heb.* vol. 79, 1906, p. 511.)
Report.

178. Zionism: a statement. (*Am. Heb.* vol. 80, 1906–7, pp. 191–194.)
With portrait. See also p. 190 (editorial comment); vol. 78, 1905–6, pp. 201–202 ("Dr Schechter on Zionism"; editorial comment). Also *J.C.* Jan. 26, 1906, p. 21.

178*a*. Professor Schechter's views on Zionism. (*J. Comment*, vol. 22, 1905–6, no. 13, pp. 7–9.)
"Authorized report." See also no. 12, p. 6 (editorial comment).

178*b*. Zionism: a statement. [*New York*]: *Federation of American Zionists*, [1906]. 15 pp. 16°.

178*c*. —— (*In his* Seminary addresses and other papers, pp. 91–104.)

178 *d.* Der zionistischer "Far-wos"; vun a ehrlichen Iden. Übersetzt vun Leon Zolotkoff. [Yiddish.] *Chicago: Press of the Daily Jewish Courier*, [1907]. 16 pp. Nar. 16°.

178 *e.* צירונידם — וואָס עס מיינט. [פון] שלמה שעכטער [translated by Ezekiel Rabbinovich]. (*Yiddishe, Dos, Folk.* [Weekly.] New York, 1915. Vol. 7, nos. 47, 48, 50.)

—— KOHLER, K. Zionism or Judaism—which? A counter statement. (*Reform Advocate.* Chicago, 1906–7. Vol. 32, pp. 847–858.)

See also *J.C.* Feb. 22, 1907, p. 15; April 19, p. 15.

—— SCHIFF, JACOB H. [Open letter to S., in reply to a letter of S., not published on account of its personal references.] (*Am. Heb.* vol. 81, 1907, p. 385.)

Declares that a true American cannot be a good Zionist.

—— —— [Second letter to S.; replying to certain criticisms made upon the first.] (*Am. Heb.* vol. 81, 1907, p. 509.)

—— SCHREIBER, E. Schechter's début as a Zionist. (*Reform Advocate.* Chicago, 1906. Vol. 31, pp. 109–110.)

1907

179. Address at the graduation exercises of the Jewish Theological Seminary, [June 2, 1907]. (*Am. Heb.* vol. 81, 1907, pp. 114–116.)

With portrait.

179 *a.* Professor Schechter on the study of Torah. (*J. Comment,* vol. 25, 1907, pp. 133–135, 145–147.)

179*b*. The problem of religious education. (*In his* Seminary addresses and other papers, pp. 105–117.)

180. [Remarks at the beginning of the term of the J.T.S.A., and comments thereon.] (*Am. Heb.* vol. 81, 1907, p. 567.)

181. [Letter addressed to the committee for organization of a local branch of the J.T.S.A. at Newark, N.J.] (*Am. Heb.* vol. 82, 1907–8, p. 88.)

1908

182. Studies in Judaism. Second series. By S. Schechter, M.A., Litt.D. *Philadelphia: Jewish Publication Society of America* [also, *London: A. and C. Black*], 1908. xi pp., 1 l., 362 pp. 8°.

Dedication: "To my wife in devotion and gratitude."

Contents: [Preface.] A hoard of Hebrew manuscripts, I. A hoard of Hebrew manuscripts, II. The study of the Bible. A glimpse of the social life of the Jews in the age of Jesus the son of Sirach. [Lecture delivered in the course of public Lectures of the J.T.S.A., 1904–5. (See also nos. 119 and 123.)] On the study of the Talmud. The memoirs of a Jewess of the seventeenth century. [Review of Die Memoiren der Glückel von Hameln, 1645–1719; hrsg. von D. Kaufmann, 1896. Printed for the first time.] Saints and saintliness. Four epistles to the Jews of England. Safed in the sixteenth century: a city of legists and mystics. [Depiction of the life of the community in its various aspects; printed for the first time.] Appendixes A and B. [New material (especially in A) from MSS. bearing on the essay "Safed".] Notes [mainly authorities for statements made in the text]. Index [prepared by Henriette Szold].

Essay on "Safed" was announced as being under way in 1895; see note following no. 86.

REVIEWS

A[BRAHAMS], I. Books and bookmen. (*J.C.* June 12, 1908, p. 18.)
See also July 3, p. 13 (announcement of American publication).

AMIEL, *pseud.* of Louis H. Levin. [Review.] (*J. Comment,* vol. 27, 1908, p. 55.)
See also pp. 38 and 54 (editorial comments).

BADT, B. Besprechung. (*M.G.W.J.* Jahrg. 53, 1909, pp. 251–256.)

DAVIES, T. W. [Review.] (*Review of Theology and Philosophy,* vol. 4, 1908–9, pp. 235–237.)

JACOBS, J. Schechter's Studies in Judaism, second series. (*Am. Heb.* vol. 82, 1907–8, p. 657.)
See also vol. 83, p. 4 (editorial comment).

L [   ]. Bücherschau. (*Mitteilungen zur jüdischen Volkskunde,* Jahrg. 12, 1909, p. 95.)

VOLZ, P. Judentum. (*Theologischer Jahresbericht,* Bd. 28, 1908, p. 167.)

See also Friedlander, J., "Studies of Judaism" (*B'nai B'rith news,* Chicago, 1916, vol. 8, no. 9, p. 2); Schulman, S., "The [Jewish Publication] Society's publications" (*American Jewish year book,* Philadelphia, 1913, pp. 131–133); same, in Jewish Publication Society of America, *Twenty-fifth anniversary* (Philadelphia, 1913), pp. 117–119; Simon, M., "Conceptions of Judaism", in *Zionism, problems and views . . .* (London [1916]), pp. 214–218. Excerpts (ser. 1–2), in *Jewish Theological Seminary of America Students' annual,* vol. 3, 1916, pp. 23–32.

182 *a.* ‏הגליל‎ (*In* ‏צפת‎. ‏במאה הט״ז‎. ‏תרגום י. יעקבי‎ ‏קובץ א‎. *Safed,* 1919, pp. 6–42 [text], 196–200 [notes]. 8°.)

183. Address [at the graduation exercises of the J.T.S.A., June 7, 1908]. (*Am. Heb.* vol. 83, 1908, pp. 129–131.)

See also *J.C.* July 10, 1908, p. 19 ("Precept and example"; extract).

183*a.* Rabbi as a personal example. (*In his* Seminary addresses and other papers, pp. 125–136.)
Last paragraph omitted; introductory paragraph added.

184. [Address at the opening session of the J.T.S.A., Oct. 20, 1908.] (*Am. Heb.* vol. 83, 1908, p. 612.)
Report.

185. Reception to Dr Schechter in Newark [at the local Branch of the J.T.S.A.]. (*Am. Heb.* vol. 84, 1908–9, p. 105.)
Remarks quoted and commented upon.

186. Lector Meir Friedmann. [Obituary.] (*Am. Heb.* vol. 84, 1908–9, pp. 147–148.)

186*a.* —— (*In his* Seminary addresses and other papers, pp. 135–143.)

186*b.* אחרי מטתו של תלמיד—חכם. [מאת] פרופ. ש. ז. שכטר.
(*In* שבלים. *New York*, 1909. Pp. 7–10. 4°.)

187. Christiànity's greatest rabbinic scholar [Charles Taylor; obituary]. (*J. Comment*, vol. 27, 1908, pp. 357–358.)

1909

188. Some aspects of rabbinic theology. By S. Schechter, M.A., Litt.D. (Cantab.). *New York: The Macmillan Co.* [also, *London: A. and C. Black*], 1909. xxii pp., 1 l., 384 pp. 8°.
Reissued, 1923. Dedication: "To Louis Marshall, Esquire, Jew and American."
Contents: [Preface.] Chap. I. Introductory. II. God and the world. III. God and Israel. IV. Election of Israel. V. The kingdom of God (invisible). VI. The visible kingdom (universal). VII. The kingdom of God (national). VIII. The

"Law". IX. The Law as personified in the literature. X. The Torah in its aspect of Law (Mizwoth). XI. The joy of the Law. XII. The Zachuth of the fathers. Imputed righteousness and imputed sin. XIII. The law of holiness and the law of goodness. XIV. Sin as rebellion. XV. The evil Yezer: the source of rebellion. XVI. Man's victory by the grace of God, over the evil Yezer created by God. XVII. Forgiveness and reconciliation with God. XVIII. Repentance: means of reconciliation. Additions and corrections. List of abbreviations and books not quoted with full title [prepared by Alexander Marx]. Index [prepared by Henriette Szold].

"The contents of this book have grown out of a course of lectures delivered at various learned centres, and a series of essays published in the *Jewish Quarterly Review*.... They are now presented to the public in an expanded form, revised and corrected, and increased by new chapters and other additional matter, amounting to about half of the bulk of this volume.... [It] represents no philosophic exposition of the body of doctrine of the Synagogue, nor does it offer a description of its system of ethics.... The task...was to give a presentation of Rabbinic opinion on a number of theological topics as offered by the Rabbinic literature, and forming an integral part of the religious consciousness of the bulk of the nation or 'Catholic Israel'" (pp. vii–viii). Excerpts, in *Jewish Theological Seminary of America Students' annual*, vol. 3, 1916, pp. 33–37.

"Among the works in preparation by Messrs T. and T. Clarke[!], of Edinburgh, there is one of exceptional interest for Jewish students. This is an 'Introduction to Rabbinical Literature' by Mr S. Schechter..." (*J.C.* Oct. 30, 1896, p. 18).

REVIEWS

[Anonymous review.] (*American Catholic Quarterly Review*, vol. 34, pp. 167–169.)

[Anonymous review.] (*Athenaeum* [London], 1909, I, p. 252.)

[Anonymous review.] (*Nation* [New York], vol. 88, pp. 308 f.)

A[BRAHAMS], I. Books and bookmen. (*J.C.* July 16, 1909, pp. 18–19.)

DAVIES, T. W. Some aspects of rabbinic theology. (*Review of Theology and Philosophy*, vol. 5, 1909–10, pp. 156–160.)

GILBERT, G. H. [Review.] (*American Journal of Theology*, vol. 14, 1910, p. 125.)

GREENE, W. B., jr. Recent literature. (*Princeton Theological Review*, vol. 8, 1910, pp. 469–474.)

JACOBS, J. Some impressions. (*Am. Heb.* vol. 84, 1908–9, pp. 359–360.)
See also p. 314.

MARGOLIS, M. L. Prof. Schechter's "Aspects of rabbinic theology." (*J. Comment*, vol. 28, 1908–9, pp. 221–223.)
See also p. 278 (editorial comment).

MONTGOMERY, J. A. [Review.] (*International Journal of Ethics*, vol. 20, pp. 111–114.)

SALKINOWITZ, G. Literarische Mitteilungen. (*Allgemeine Zeitung des Judentums.* Berlin, 1909. Jahrg. 73, p. 168.)

See also Box, C. H., "Jewish environment of early Christianity" (*Expositor*, ser. 8, vol. 12, 1916, pp. 6–7, 9). See also *J.C.* Jan. 15, 1895, p. 13 (reference); Feb. 22, 1895, pp. 5–6 (editorial, quoting S. in refutation of A. J. Balfour's statement that of all theistic systems Christianity was the most satisfying); April 10, 1903, p. 26 (R. T. Herford, in his articles on the "Religion of the Rabbis", in the *Inquirer*, "makes very full and very able use of Dr Schechter's articles on Rabbinic Theology").

188 a. Das Gesetz der Heiligkeit und Liebe. [Translation of ch. XIII: The law of holiness and the law of goodness.] (*Jahrbuch für jüdische Geschichte und Literatur*. Berlin, 1912. Bd. 15, pp. 146–162.)

189. Moritz Steinschneider. [Obituary.] (*In* American Jewish Historical Society. Publications. [*Baltimore*], 1909. No. 17, pp. 226–231.)

189 a. —— [*Baltimore*], 1909. 5 pp. 8°.

190. Abraham Lincoln. (*Am. Heb.* vol. 84, 1908–9, pp. 390–394.)

Lecture delivered at the J.T.S.A., Feb. 11, 1909. See also p. 425 ("Lincoln as mystic"; comment by "An Inconstant Reader"). Also *J. Comment*, vol. 28, 1908–9, pp. 319 (excerpt) and 326 (editorial comment).

190*a*. Abraham Lincoln. Memorial address delivered at the Lincoln centennial celebration of the Jewish Theological Seminary of America. By S. Schechter, President. *New York: J.T.S.A.* 1909. 29 pp. 8°.

190*b*. —— (*In his* Seminary addresses and other papers, pp. 145–168.)

190*c*. —— (*In* Hertz, E., Abraham Lincoln.... *New York*, 1927. Pp. 383–400. 8°.)

191. Prof. Benno Badt. [Obituary.] (*Am. Heb.* vol. 85, 1909, p. 8.)

191*a*. —— (*In his* Seminary addresses and other papers, pp. 169–172.)

192. Address to Seminary graduates [June 6, 1909]. (*Am. Heb.* vol. 85, 1909, pp. 139–141.)

192*a*. President Schechter's address to the graduates. (*J. Comment*, vol. 29, 1909, pp. 145–148.)

193. [Address at the opening session of the J.T.S.A., Oct. 11, 1909.] (*Am. Heb.* vol. 85, 1909, p. 599.)
Condensed report.

194. Prof. Schechter's address [at the dedication of the new Talmud Torah building at Baltimore, Md.]. (*J. Comment*, vol. 29, 1909, pp. 56–57.)
Part only.

1910

195. Documents of Jewish sectaries. Volumes 1–2....
Edited...by S. Schechter, M.A., Litt.D.
(Cantab.), President of the Jewish Theological
Seminary of America in New York. *Cambridge:
at the University Press*, 1910. Sq. 4°.

Vol. 1. Fragments of a Zadokite work. Edited from Hebrew
manuscripts in the Cairo Genizah collection now in the possession of the University Library, Cambridge, and provided with
an English translation, introduction and notes. [Index to Bible,
Apocrypha and rabbinical works in the notes (prepared by
Joseph B. Abrahams).] 3 p. l., (i)vi–lxiv, 20 pp., 1 l., 2 facs.
MS. T-S. 10 K. 6 [MS. A]; T-S. 16. 311 [MS. B].

Vol. 2. קונטרסים מספר המצות לענן. Fragments of the
Book of the commandments by Anan. Edited from Hebrew
manuscripts in the Cairo Genizah collection now in the possession
of the University Library, Cambridge, and provided with a short
introduction and notes. 3 p. l., (v)–vi, 50 pp. MS. T-S. 16.
359–365 [MS. A]; T-S. 16. 366 [MS. B]; T-S. 16. 367 a
[MS. C]; T-S. 16. 367 b [MS. D].

"The two groups of fragments...were all discovered in the
Cairo Genizah....[The title of vol. 1] was supplied by me on
a hypothesis. [The title of vol. 2] was also supplied by me, but
which may be accepted as a certainty....The risk of giving a
translation of [vol. 1]...was great indeed....This risk I felt
not less when writing the Introduction and the Notes to the
text, but I preferred to be blamed for my mistakes and be
corrected, than be praised for my prudence of non-committal,
which policy I do not always think worthy of a student.... The
divisions into paragraphs were supplied by me, so as to enable the
student to form some notion of the variety of matter touched
upon in our fragments.... Much less was the labour spent upon
the second volume...." The first public utterance "on a newly-
discovered document of an old Jewish sect" was made by S.
before the Society of Biblical Literature and Exegesis at its
annual meeting, Dec. 30–31, 1902. See *J. Comment*, vol. 16,
no. 12, p. 11. Dedication: "To the Honourable Jacob H.
Schiff."

SOLOMON SCHECHTER

REVIEWS

[Anonymous.] Ein neu entdecktes jüdisches Dokument zum Urchristentum. (*Frankfurter Zeitung*, Dec. 15, 1910, no. 346.)

[Anonymous.] New Christian Scriptures? (*Harper's Weekly*, Jan. [?], 1911, p. 19.)

[Anonymous.] Schechters Sekten-Dokument. (*Israelit.* Frankfurt-a.-M., 1910. Jahrg. 51, no. 51, p. 14.)

[Anonymous.] Important Jewish manuscript older than Gospels. (*Times* [New York] *Sunday Magazine Section*, Jan. 1, 1911.)

A[brahams], I. Books and bookmen. (*J.C.* Dec. 9, 1910, p. 20.)

—— [Reference.] (*J.C.* Sept. 29, 1911, p. 22.)

—— A note on two comments. (*J.C.* Oct. 20, 1911, p. 22.) A reply to G. Margoliouth's communication of Oct. 6.

Adler, N. The Sadducean Christians of Damascus. (*Athenaeum* [London], Feb. 4, 1911, p. 128.)
A communication, with reference to G. Margoliouth's review in *Athenaeum*, Nov. 26, 1910; reprinted in *Am. Heb.* vol. 88, 1910–11, p. 492; see also p. 500 (editorial comment). See also *J.C.* Feb. 17, 1911, p. 22 (note).

Bacher, W. Zu Schechters neuestem Geniza-Funde. (*Zeitschrift für hebraeische Bibliographie*, Jahrg. 15, 1911, pp. 13–26.) See also *J.C.* May 5, 1911, p. 22 (notice).

Barnes, W. E. Fresh light on Maccabean times. (*Journal of Theological Studies*, vol. 12, 1911, pp. 301–303.)

Blau, L. A válás, a polygamia és a testvér leányával való házasság a czadokita iratban. (*Magyar-Zsidó Szemle*, évf. 30, 1913, pp. 209–213.)

Boehl, F. M. T. Neu gefundene Urkunden einer messianischen Sekte in syrisch-palästinischen Judentum. [With German translation of the "Documents".] (*Theologisch-tijdschrift*, vol. 46, 1912, pp. 1–35, 93.)

Bousset, W. [Review.] (*Theologische Rundschau*, 1915, pp. 51–58.)

Buechler, A. Schechter's "Jewish sectaries" [vol. 1]. (*J.Q.R.*, new ser., vol. 3, 1912–13, pp. 429–485.) See no. 228.

62

CHAJES, H. P. I frammenti d'un libro sadduceo. (*Rivista Israelitica*, anno 7, 1910, pp. 203–213.)

—— Ancora dei frammenti d'un libro sadduceo. (*Rivista Israelitica*, anno 8, 1911, pp. 1–7.)

CHARLES, R. H. Fragments of a Zadokite work; translated from the Cambridge Hebrew text, and edited with introduction, notes and indexes. *Oxford*, 1912.
See Preface and Introduction. Reprinted in his edition of *The Apocrypha and Pseudepigrapha of the Old Testament in English*, Oxford, 1913, vol. 2, pp. 785–834.

D[AICHES], S. A "Zadokite" work [edited by R. H. Charles]. (*J.C.* Dec. 13, 1912, pp. 34–35.)

EISLER, R. The Sadoqite book of the new covenant: its date and origin. (*In* Occident and Orient....Gaster anniversary volume, *London*, [1936], pp. 110–143.)

FOAKES-JACKSON, F. J. and LAKE, K. The Covenanters of Damascus. (*In their* The beginnings of Christianity, pt. 1, vol. 1, *London*, 1920, pp. 97–101.)

GINZBERG, L. Eine unbekannte jüdische Sekte. (*M.G.W.J.* Jahrg. 55, 1911, pp. 666–698; Jahrg. 56, 1912, pp. 33–48, 285–307, 417–448, 546–566; Jahrg. 57, 1913, pp. 153–176, 284–308, 394–418, 666–696; Jahrg. 58, 1914, pp. 16–48, 143–177, 395–429.)

—— —— New York, 1922.
Reviewed by F. Perles, in *Orientalistische Literaturzeitung*, vol. 15, 1922, cols. 259–260.

GRESSMANN, H. [Review.] (*Internationale Wochenschrift für Wissenschaft, Kunst und Technik*, vol. 5, 1911, no. 9.)

—— Anzeige. (*Z.D.M.G.* Bd. 66, 1912, pp. 491–503.)
His previous standpoint G. is now obliged "in einzelnen Punkten [zu] korrigieren".

HOELSCHER, G. Zur Frage nach Alter und Herkunft der sog. Damaskusschrift. (*Zeitschrift für neutestamentliche Wissenschaft*, Bd. 28, 1929, pp. 21–46.)
In connection with the publication of F. F. Hvidberg.

HVIDBERG, F. F. Menigheden af den nye pagti Damaskus. *Kjöbenhavn*, 1928.

[JACOBS, J.] Dr Schechter's new "find". [Editorial comment.] (*Am. Heb.* vol. 88, 1910–11, pp. 226–227.)

KOHLER, K. Dositheus, the Samaritan heresiarch, and his relations to Jewish and Christian doctrines and sects. (*American Journal of Theology*, vol. 15, 1911, pp. 404–435.)
Also separately. See also *J.C.* Sept. 8, 1911, p. 22 (notice).

LAGRANGE, M.-J. La secte juive de la nouvelle alliance au pays de Damas. [With translation of the "Documents".] (*Revue Biblique internationale*, tom. 9, 1912, pp. 213–240, 321–360.)

LANDAUER, S. [Review.] (*Theologische Literaturzeitung*, Jahrg. 37, 1912, cols. 261–264.)
See also Jahrg. 36, 1911, col. 220.

LESZYNSKY, R. H. Observations sur les *Fragments of a Zadokite work*. (*R.E.J.* tom. 62, 1911, pp. 190–196.)

LÉVI, I. Un écrit sadducéen antérieur à la destruction du temple. [Discussion, translation of the "Documents", and notes.] (*R.E.J.* tom. 61, 1911, pp. 161–205.)

—— Notes sur les Observations de M. [R.] Leszynsky. (*R.E.J.* tom. 62, 1911, pp. 197–200.)

—— Document relatif à la "Communauté des fils de Sadoc". (*R.E.J.* tom. 65, 1913, pp. 24–31.)

—— Le tétragramme et l'écrit sadokite de Damas. (*R.E.J.* tom. 68, 1914, pp. 119–121.)

LIGHTLEY, J. W. The recently discovered Zadokite fragments. (*London Quarterly Review*, vol. 123, 1915, pp. 15–31.)

MARGOLIOUTH, G. The Sadducean Christians of Damascus. (*Athenaeum* [London], Nov. 26, 1910, pp. 657–659.)

—— The Sadducean Christians of Damascus. [Reply to E. N. Adler.] (*Athenaeum* [London], March 4, 1911, p. 249.)

—— The two Zadokite messiahs. (*Journal of Theological Studies*, vol. 12, 1911, pp. 446–450.)

—— The Zadoke problem. (*J.C.* Oct. 6, 1911, p. 21.)
A communication, referring to I. Abrahams' "brief reference" of Sept. 29.

—— The Zadokites once more. (*Jewish Review*. London, 1911–12. Vol. 2, pp. 361–369.)

MARGOLIOUTH, G. The Sadducean Christians of Damascus. (*Expositor*, ser. 8, vol. 2, 1911, pp. 499–517; ser. 8, vol. 3, 1912, pp. 213–234.)

—— The Sadducean Christians of Damascus. [Reply to W. H. Ward.] (*Bibliotheca Sacra*, vol. 69, 1912, pp. 421–437.)

—— The calendar, the Sabbath and the marriage law in the Geniza-Zadokite document. (*Expository Times*, vol. 23, 1912, pp. 362–365.)

—— Fragments of a Zadokite work. (*International Journal of Apocrypha*, no. 37 [or, ser. 10], 1914, pp. 36–37.) Takes issue with R. H. Charles.

MARGOLIS, M. L. Dr Schechter's great discovery. (*J. Comment*, vol. 33, 1910–11, pp. 217–219.)

MARMORSTEIN, A. Eine unbekannte jüdische Sekte. (*Theologisch Tijdschrift*, 1918, pp. 92–122.)

MEYER, E. Die Gemeinde des neuen Bundes im Lande Damaskus. Eine jüdische Schrift aus der Seleukidenzeit. (*In* Preussische Akademie der Wissenschaften. Phil.-hist. Kl. Abhandl. Jahrg. 1919, no. 9.)

MONTGOMERY, J. A. A lost Jewish sect. (*Biblical World*, vol. 38, 1911, pp. 373–383.)

MOORE, G. F. The Covenanters of Damascus; a hitherto unknown Jewish sect. (*Harvard Theological Review*, vol. 4, 1911, pp. 330–377.) See also his *Judaism in the first centuries of the Christian era* (Cambridge [Mass.], 1927), vol. 1, pp. 200–204.

POZNANSKI, S. [Review of vols. 1 and 2.] (*Jewish Review*. London, 1911–12. Vol. 2, pp. 273–281.)

—— More about Schechter's "Fragments of a Zadokite work". (*Jewish Review*. London, 1911–12. Vol. 2, pp. 443–446.) A reply to G. Margoliouth in *Jewish Review*, vol. 2, pp. 361–369.

RIESSLER, P. Sadokitisches Werk. (*In his* Altjüdisches Schrifttum ausserhalb der Bibel. *Augsburg*, 1928. Pp. 920–941 [translation], 1323–1325 [notes].)

SEGAL, M. H. Notes on "Fragments of a Zadokite work". (*J.Q.R.* new ser., vol. 2, 1911–12, pp. 133–141.)

SEGAL, M. H. Additional notes on "Fragments of a Zadokite work". (*J.Q.R.* new ser., vol. 3, 1912–13, pp. 301–311.)

—— ‏ספר ברית־דמשק. עם מבוא והערות מאת משה צבי סגל‎

‏(השלח)‎, vol. 26, 1912, pp. 390–406, 483–506.)

STAERK, W. Die jüdische Gemeinde des neuen Bundes in Damaskus. (*In* Beiträge zur Förderung christlicher Theologie, XXVII 3, 1922.)

STRACK, H. L. Die israelitische Gemeinde des "neuen Bundes" in Damaskus. (*Reformation* [Berlin], vol. 10, pp. 105–108.)

[WARD, W. H. ?] Mr [G.] Margoliouth's dream. (*Independent* [New York], vol. 71, 1911, pp. 555–556.)

WARD, W. H. The "Zadokite" documents. (*Bibliotheca Sacra*, vol. 68, 1911, pp. 429–456.)

WEIR, T. H. Survey of recent archaeology in relation to Palestine. [Review of vol. 1 and 2.] (*Review of Theology & Philosophy*, vol. 8, 1912–13, pp. 7–8.)

WESTPHAL, G. Die Inschrift aus der Kairoer Geniza [vol. 1]. (*Theologischer Jahresbericht*, Bd. 31, Hälfte 1, 1911, pp. 238–239.)

WIERNIK, P. ‏א אידישער דאָקומענט פון דער צייט פון‎ ‏צווייטען בית המקדש‎. (*Amerikaner*. [Yiddish weekly.] New York, 1911. Vol. 9, no. 20, pp. 1–2.)

196. Address to the graduating class of the Jewish Theological Seminary [June 5, 1910]. (*Am. Heb.* vol. 87, 1910, pp. 133–134.)

196a. President Schechter's address. (*J. Comment*, vol. 31, 1910, pp. 133–134, 137–138.)

196b. The test the rabbi should apply. (*In his* Seminary addresses and other papers, pp. 195–205.)

197. [American Judaism. Interview on the eve of his sailing for South Africa.] (*Globe* [New York], June 25, 1910.)

197*a*. —— (*Am. Heb.* vol. 87, 1910, p. 214.)

198. [American Judaism. Interview upon his arrival in England.] (*J.C.* July 8, 1910, pp. 18, 21.) With portrait.

198*a*. —— (*Am. Heb.* vol. 87, 1910, pp. 286–287.)

—— MORAIS, H.S. Professor Schechter and American Jewry. (*J.C.* Aug. 26, 1910, p. 22.)

199. Some impressions of South African Jewry. Interview. (*J.C.* Dec. 30, 1910, p. 18.)

199*a*. —— (*Am. Heb.* vol. 88, 1910–11, p. 309.)

200. Is a reconciliation between reform and orthodoxy possible? [Symposium.] (*Jewish Daily News* [New York], 1910, no. 67 [Jubilee number; English section].)

201. Editorial announcement. [By Cyrus Adler and S. Schechter.] (*J.Q.R.* new ser., vol. 1, 1910–11, pp. 1–4.)
See *J.C.* July 29, 1910, p. 18. S. was co-editor of the new series of the *J.Q.R.* from 1910–1915.

202. The beginnings of Jewish "Wissenschaft". (*Jewish Review.* London, 1910–11. Vol. 1, pp. 295–312.)
"A great part of the matter...is taken from the introductory lecture to a course of lectures on the Genizah, delivered in the spring term of 1910 at the Dropsie College." See *J.C.* Nov. 11, 1910, p. 23.

202*a*. —— (*In his* Seminary addresses and other papers, pp. 173–193.)
Some sentences omitted (compare p. 306 in *Jewish Review* with p. 186 in *Seminary addresses*); essay also shows a few verbal changes (e.g. "reform tendencies" and "Rationalism", in place of "Reformers" and "Reform"). See p. xiii of Preface to *Seminary addresses*.

1911

203. מכילתא לדברים פרשת ראה. (*In* Festschrift zu Israel Lewy's siebzigsten Geburtstag. *Breslau*, 1911. [Heb. sec.], pp. 187–192. 8°.)

Paged also i–vi. Preface signed, שניאור זלמן שעכטער ב"ר יצחק הכהן ז"ל. Genizah fragment; 2 leaves (much defaced, and not continuous); twelfth century.

203a. —— [*Breslau: M. and H. Marcus* (at H. Itzkowski in Berlin), 1911.] vi pp. 8°.
Paged also 187–192.

REVIEW

GINZBERG, L. Bibliographie. (*R.E.J.* tom. 67, 1914, p. 135.)

204. The remnant of youth in Israel. (*Am. Heb.* vol. 88, 1910–11, pp. 636–637.)
Letter written while abroad and read at the B'nai Jeshurun congregational meeting, March 30, 1911.

204a. Communication from Professor Solomon Schechter. (*In* New York, N.Y. Congregation B'nai Jeshurun. Meeting of Congregation B'nai Jeshurun, held...March 30, 1911. [*New York*, 1911.] Pp. 19–22.)

205. [European Judaism. Interview upon his return to the U.S.] (*Am. Heb.* vol. 89, 1911, p. 7.)
See also p. 14 (editorial comment).

205a. President Schechter's impressions of his journey. (*J. Comment*, vol. 34, 1911, p. 50.)
With portrait.

205b. —— (*J.C.* May 19, 1911, p. 11.)

206. Address to Seminary graduates [June 4, 1911]. (*Am. Heb.* vol. 89, 1911, pp. 153–154.)

207. The building of altars. (*Am. Heb.* vol. 89, 1911, pp. 625–626.)
Extract from address at the dedication of Ohab Sholom Synagogue, Newark, N.J.

208. [Address at the opening session of the J.T.S.A., Oct. 17, 1911.] (*Am. Heb.* vol. 89, 1911, p. 773.)
Part only.

209. Oppressed Russian Jews. Security of dividends but not of life. (*Times* [New York], Oct. 12, 1911.)
Letter to the editor.

209 a. —— (*J.C.* Nov. 10, 1911, p. 10.)

210. Message from Professor Schechter. (*J. Comment*, vol. 33, 1910–11, pp. 216–217.)
A communication, read at the induction of Rabbi J. L. Magnes.

1912

211. The Beth Hamidrash. (*Am. Heb.* vol. 90, 1911–12, pp. 579–580.)
Address delivered at the dedication of Dropsie College building, Philadelphia, March 11, 1912.

211 a. —— (*J.C.* April 5, 1912, p. 11.)

211 b. —— (*In his* Seminary addresses and other papers, pp. 207–215.)

212. [Address at the 25th anniversary of the founding of the Philadelphia Branch of the Jewish Theological Seminary Association, April 21, 1912.] (*Am. Heb.* vol. 90, 1911–12, p. 788.)

213. The duty of the rabbi. Address to the graduating class of the Jewish Theological Seminary, [June 2, 1912]. (*Am. Heb.* vol. 91, 1912, pp. 147–149.)

213*a*. President Schechter's commencement address. (*J. Comment*, vol. 39, 1912, pp. 129–131.)

213*b*. The duty of the rabbi. (*J.C.* June 21, 1912, pp. 20–21.)
With portrait.

213*c*. Humility and self-sacrifice as the qualifications of the rabbi. (*In his* Seminary addresses and other papers, pp. 217–228.)

214. An unknown Khazar document. (*J.Q.R.* new ser., vol. 3, 1912–13, pp. 181–219.)

Genizah MS. in the Cambridge University Library; two leaves; "affording quite new matter. It was discovered several years ago, but was only properly examined within the last few months." Introduction; Hebrew text and facsimile; English translation; map showing the kingdom of the Khazars (from Spruner-Menke, *Hand-Atlas für die Geschichte des Mittelalters*, Gotha, 1880, 3rd ed.).

REVIEW

KAHANA, D. מָקוֹר חָדָשׁ לְתוֹלְדוֹת—הַכּוּזָרִים. (השלח, Bd. 28, 1913, pp. 523–529.)

215. Old manuscripts reveal a lost Jewish kingdom. (*Times* [New York], Nov. 17, 1912, pp. 3–4 [Magazine section?].)

Full description, English translation of the document, facsimiles and map. With portrait. See *J. Comment*, vol. 40, p. 77 (notice). [It may be noted in this connection that copies of the rare little book קול מבשר (Constantinople, 1577), containing Ḥasdai Ibn Shaprut's letter to the Khazar king, are in the Hebrew Union College Library, Cincinnati, Ohio, and in the Library of the J.T.S.A.]

1913

216. [Address at the banquet concluding the exercises of the 25th anniversary of the founding of the J.P.S.A.] (*In* Jewish Publication Society of America. Twenty-fifth anniversary. *Philadelphia*, 1913. Pp. 158–163.)
Part only.

216*a*. —— (*American Jewish year book.* 1913–1914, pp. 172–177.)

217. Letter to the convention. (*In* Intercollegiate Menorah Association. Report of the constituent convention...held at the University of Chicago, January 1, 2 and 3, 1913.... [*New York*], 1913. Pp. 29–30. 8°.)

217*a*. —— (*In* Intercollegiate Menorah Association. The Menorah movement.... History, purposes, activities. *Ann Arbor, Michigan*, 1914. Pp. 67–68. 8°.)

218. Midrash fragment. (*In* Studies in Jewish literature; issued in honor of Kaufmann Kohler. *Berlin*, 1913. Pp. 260–265. 4°.)
Genizah fragment; 1 leaf. Represents a "lost Midrash" which "may possibly be the Yelamdenu". It "gives a long Derasha interpreting certain verses in Job to refer to the Generation of the Deluge". See *J.Q.R.* new ser., vol. 5, 1914–15, p. 497 (J. H. Greenstone suggests "a slight correction in text"). See also Ginzberg, L., *Genizah studies in memory of Doctor Solomon Schechter* (New York, 1928), vol. 1, Introduction.

218*a*. —— [*Berlin: G. Reimer*, 1913.] 7 pp. 8°.
No title-page. 25 copies printed for private distribution.

219. The United Synagogue of America. (*Am. Heb.* vol. 92, 1912–13, pp. 487–489.)

Address delivered at the convention held to inaugurate a "United Synagogue of America", Feb. 23, 1913, outlining the policy of the organization.

219*a*. —— (*J. Comment*, vol. 40, 1912–13, p. 259.)

219*b*. —— (*In* United Synagogue of America. Report, 1913. *New York*, 1913. Pp. 14–23.)

220. [Address delivered at the graduating exercises of the J.T.S.A., June 8, 1913.] (*Am. Heb.* vol. 93, 1913, pp. 171–172.)

220*a*. The assistance of the public. (*In his* Seminary addresses and other papers, pp. 229–237.)

221. The election of Chief Rabbi. Dr Schechter's recommendation [of Joseph H. Hertz for the post]. (*J.C.* Feb. 14, 1913, p. 12.)

Letter to the Electoral College. See also Feb. 21, p. 30 (reference and portrait); March 14, p. 13 (reference).

221*a*. Professor Schechter and Dr Hertz. (*J. Comment*, vol. 40, 1912–13, p. 256.)

1914

222. Wilhelm Bacher. [Obituary.] (*In* American Jewish Historical Society. Publications. [*Baltimore*], 1914. No. 22, pp. 203–206. 8°.)

222*a*. —— [*Baltimore*], 1914. 4 pp. 8°.

223. הלכות על סדר הפרשיות. מאת ז. שעכטער. [Edited with a short introduction.] (*In* Festschrift zum siebzigsten Geburtstage D. Hoffmann's. *Berlin*, 1914. [Heb. sec.], pp. 261–266. 4°.)

Paged also i–vi. Genizah fragment. Inclines to identify the author with a certain Aba, or Rabbah, or Raba, pupil of Yehudai Gaon.

223*a*. —— *Berlin*, 1914. 6 pp. 4°.

224. Address [at the celebration of the conclusion of the Bible translation, Feb. 10, 1914]. (*Am. Heb.* vol. 94, 1913–14, pp. 448–449.)

225. [Address at the second annual convention of the United Synagogue of America, March 22, 1914.] (*Am. Heb.* vol. 94, 1913–14, pp. 615–616.)

Presidential address.

225*a*. —— (*In* United Synagogue of America. Report of the second annual meeting. *New York*, 1914. Pp. 13–17.)

226. Address to graduate rabbis, [June 7, 1914]. (*Am. Heb.* vol. 95, 1914, pp. 175–176.)

226*a*. —— President Schechter's message. (*J. Comment*, vol. 43, 1914, pp. 127–128.)

226*b*. The duty of the "rabbi". (*J.C.* June 26, 1914, p. 23.)

"Chief portion" only.

226*c*. —— (*Jewish World* [London], June 24, 1914, pp. 19–20.)

226*d*. Address to graduate rabbis. (*Jewish Theological Seminary of America Students' annual*, vol. 2, 1915, pp. 38–42.)

227. Zionism. (*J.C.* Jan. 2, 1914, p. 49.)

Report of address delivered at Cincinnati, O. The address was translated into Yiddish by Dr Landman, a Cincinnati physician, and published in the *Yiddishe Folk* (N.Y.).

228. Reply to Dr [A.] Büchler's review of Schechter's "Jewish sectaries". (*J.Q.R.* new ser., vol. 4, 1913–14, pp. 449–474.)

229. [Interview about Stephen Langdon's discovery of a Sumerian epic of paradise, the flood and the fall of man supposed to antedate the version in Genesis by at least a thousand years.] (*Times* [New York], June 25, 1914, p. 3, col. 3.)

230. [Letter to the editor; regarding S. Langdon's discovery.] (*Times* [New York], June 26, 1914, p. 12, col. 6.)

1915

231. Seminary addresses and other papers. By S. Schechter, M.A., Litt.D., President of the Jewish Theological Seminary of America. *Cincinnati: Ark Publishing Co.* 1915. xiv pp., 1 l., 253 pp., 1 port. 8°.

Dedicated "To Cyrus Adler, President of the Dropsie College, colleague and friend."

Contents: [Preface.] The emancipation of Jewish science. The charter of the Seminary. Higher criticism—higher anti-Semitism. The Seminary as a witness. Spiritual honeymoons. Rebellion against being a problem. The reconciliation of Israel. Altar building in America. Zionism: a statement. The problem of religious education. Moritz Steinschneider. Rabbi as a personal example. Lector Meir Friedmann. Abraham Lincoln. Benno Badt. The beginnings of Jewish "Wissenschaft". The test the rabbi should apply. The Beth Hamidrash. Humility and self-sacrifice as the qualifications of the rabbi. The assistance of the public. His Majesty's opposition. [Address at the dedication of the new buildings of the Hebrew Union College, Jan. 22, 1913; printed for the first time.] "Lovingkindness and truth."

Extracts in *Jewish Theological Seminary of America Students' annual*, vol. 3, 1916, pp. 38–43.

REVIEWS

[Anonymous review.] (*Nation* [New York], vol. 103, 1916, p. 518.)

A[BRAHAMS], I. [Review.] (*J.C.* Nov. 5, 1915, p. 27.)

E[LBOGEN], I. [Review.] (*Zeitschrift für hebraeische Bibliographie*, Jahrg. 9, 1916, p. 18.)

JACOBS, J. Dr Schechter's Addresses. (*Am. Heb.* vol. 97, 1915, p. 576.)

ROSENBERG, S. [Review.] (*Hebrew Union College Monthly.* Cincinnati, O., 1915–16. Vol. 2, p. 172.)

The London *Times Weekly* also published a review.

232. Letter [of congratulation] to Harry Z. Gordon, Managing Editor. (*Jewish Theological Seminary of America Students' annual*, vol. 2, 1915, p. 9.)

233. Address [at the graduation exercises of the J.T.S.A., June 6, 1915]. (*Am. Heb.* vol. 97, 1915, pp. 135–136.)

With portrait. Last public address. Introductory paragraphs omitted. See also p. 140. Extract in New York *Times*, June 7, 1915, p. 4, col. 3. See *J. Comment*, vol. 45, 1915, p. 138 (editorial comment). See also *Jewish World* [London], June 30, 1915, pp. 12–13 (report).

233a. "Lovingkindness and truth." (*In his* Seminary addresses and other papers, pp. 245–253.)

233b. —— (*Jewish Theological Seminary of America Students' annual*, vol. 3, 1916, pp. 17–22.)

234. [Letter of congratulation to the Intercollegiate Menorah Association upon launching its Journal.] (*Menorah Journal.* New York, 1915. Vol. 1, p. 11.)

235. An appeal from the grave to American Israel. By S. Schechter. *New York*, 1915. 8 pp. 8°.

Text, pp. 5–7. "At the suggestion of Mr Nathan Straus, the late Prof. Schechter wrote the...appeal for funds [for Jewish war sufferers] under date of September 2, 1915. It is now [Dec. 24] published for the first time, and it is a voice from the grave calling upon the Jews of America to do their duty" (p. 3).

235a. —— (*Am. Heb.* vol. 98, 1915–16, no. 7 [Supplement], p. 16.)

235b. —— (*J.C.* Jan. 14, 1916, p. 12.)

235c. —— (*Sentinel* [Chicago], vol. 22, 1916, no. 6, pp. 6, 9.)

236. תורה נביאים וכתובים. The Holy Scriptures according to the Masoretic text. A new translation, with the aid of previous versions and with constant consultation of Jewish authorities. *Philadelphia: The Jewish Publication Society of America*, 5677—1917. xv, 1136 pp. 12°.

Board of Editors: S. Schechter, C. Adler, J. Jacobs (representing the Jewish Publication Society of America), K. Kohler, D. Philipson, S. Schulman (representing the Central Conference of American Rabbis); Editor-in-chief: M. L. Margolis. Begun in 1908; completed in 1915. "For one year Professor Israel Friedlaender acted as a member of the Board in the stead of Doctor Schechter" (*Preface*, p. vi).

237. Schechteriana. By Frank I. Schechter. (*Menorah Journal*. New York, 1922. Vol. 8, pp. 179–186.)

Paper read at the annual meeting of the American Jewish Historical Society. Extracts from letters of S. to his wife, to I. Zangwill, C. Adler, Dr S. Solis-Cohen, M. Sulzberger, and one from Reginald Henriquez to S.

BIBLIOGRAPHY

237*a*. —— (*J.C.* Nov. 10, 1922, pp. 20–21.)

238. Studies in Judaism. Third series. By S. Schechter, M.A., Litt.D. *Philadelphia: The Jewish Publication Society of America,* 1924. 3 p. l., (i) vi–vii, 336 pp. 8°.

Posthumously edited by Alexander Marx and Frank I. Schechter.

Contents: [Foreword by the editors.] Jewish saints in mediaeval Germany. [A lecture delivered at Temple Beth El, New York, about 1903; printed for the first time.] "As others saw him." A retrospect, A.D. 54 [by Joseph Jacobs (*London,* 1895); a review]. Abraham Geiger. [Review of Abraham Geiger, Leben und Lebenswerk (Berlin, 1910); printed for the first time.] Leopold Zunz. [Prize-essay; written in 1889 for the Jewish Ministers' Association, New York; printed for the first time. (See *J.C.* Jan. 3, 1890, p. 6.)] On the study of the Talmud. [A critique of Edersheim, *Life and times of Jesus the Messiah* (London, 1883).] The Talmud. [An encyclopaedical survey.] Notes on lectures on Jewish philanthropy. [Delivered before the students of the J.T.S.A., 1914–15; printed for the first time from the notes taken by Jacob Bosniak, and other students, collated with the notebook of S.] Notes. [With up-to-date additions by the editors.] Index. [Prepared by I. George Dobsevage.]

REVIEWS

L[EVY], S. About books. (*J.C.* March 6, 1925, p. 18.)
PERLES, F. [Review.] (*R.E.J.* tom. 80, 1925, pp. 106–108.)

239. DAVIDSON, ISRAEL, *editor*. לקט מכתבים מחכמי ישראל לשזח"ה. (*In* Studies in Jewish bibliography and related subjects in memory of Abraham Solomon Freidus. *New York,* 1929. [Heb. sec.], pp. 1–14.)

Nos. 15–22 are Schechter's letters to S. J. Halberstam.

240. [Letters to Philip Cowen.] (*In* Cowen, P.,
Memoirs of an American Jew. *New York*,
1932. Pp. 377–381. 8°.)

With portrait. Letter 1, dated Cambridge, July 9, 1900,
with reference to his coming to New York; 2, in extract, dated
Dec. 26, 1898, in answer to the question as to his views on a
synod; 3, introducing Rev. Joseph Mayor Asher; 4, dated
Ramsgate, March 19, 1902, pertaining to his removal from
England to the U.S.

APPENDIX

LIFE AND PERSONALITY

I

STUDIES AND APPRECIATIONS

1. ABELSON, ALTER. Solomon Schechter. [A poem in his memory.] (*In* Friedlander, Joseph. Standard book of Jewish verse. *New York*, 1917. Pp. 736–737. 12°.)

2. A[BRAHAMS], I[SRAEL]. Death of Schechter. (*J.C.* Nov. 26, 1915, pp. 16, 22–23.)

2 *a.* —— —— (*Reform Advocate.* Chicago, 1915–16. Vol. 50, pp. 730–735.)

3. ABRAHAMS, JOSEPH B. The Jewish Theological Seminary. [Portrait.] (*New Era.* New York, 1903–4. Vol. 4, no. 2, pp. 1–10.)

4. ADLER, CYRUS. Jewish colleges in the United States. [Introductory address at the inauguration of S. as President of the J.T.S.A.] Official report. (*J. Comment*, vol. 16, 1902–3, p. 9.)

4 *a.* —— Address. (*In* Jewish Theological Seminary of America. Biennial report, 1902–4. *New York*, 1906. Pp. 81–83. 8°.)

5. —— Solomon Schechter. A biographical sketch. [Plate and portrait.] (*American Jewish year book*, 5677, pp. 25–67. 12°.)

5 *a.* —— —— [*Philadelphia: The Jewish Publication Society of America*, 1917.] 45 pp. Sq. 8°.

Repr. *American Jewish year book*, 1916.

6. —— A tribute to Schechter. (*Menorah Journal.* New York, 1916. Vol. 2, pp. 6–7.)

Delivered informally at the "Scholars' Evening", Fourth Annual Menorah Convention, Dec. 28, 1915.

7. AMERICAN HEBREW. Dr Schechter arrives. [Account of his arrival in New York; with short biography, and description of his physique and manner.] (Vol. 70, 1901–2, pp. 657–658.)

8. —— Persons talked about [S. Schechter]. (Vol. 87, 1910, p. 108.)

9. —— Solomon Schechter. [Obituary.] (Vol. 98, 1916, p. 250.)

10. BADT-STRAUSS, BERTA. Solomon Schechter, Forscher und Führer. (*Morgen, Der.* Berlin, 1933. Jahrg. 9, no. 4, pp. 274–276.)

11. BARUCH, S., *pseud.* of A. S. Oko. Homage to Solomon Schechter. [Portrait.] (*Menorah Journal.* New York, 1937. Vol. 25, no. 2, pp. 151–156.)

12. BENTWICH, NORMAN. Solomon Schechter. [With a foreword by F. C. Burkitt.] *London: G. Allen and Unwin, Ltd.* [1931]. 4 p. l., (1)14–59(1) pp. 16°. (The Arthur Davis memorial lecture.)

13. BLOCH, JOSHUA. Prof. Solomon Schechter. [*Cincinnati, O.,* 1915.] 13 pp. 8°.

Repr. *Hebrew Union College Monthly*, nos. 4–5. Only first part is reprinted from no. 4; no. 5 does not contain part 2 of essay.

14. ——Prof. Shneiur Zalman Schechter. [Hebrew.] (*Sefer Hashanah. The American Hebrew year book*; edited by M. Ribalow and S. Bernstein. New York, 1935. Pp. —? 8°.)

14*a*. —— [*New York*], 1935. 11(1) pp. 8°.
Repr. *Sefer Hashana.*

15. CAMBRIDGE REVIEW. Dr Schechter. [Obituary.]
(Vol. 37, 1915–16, p. 112.)

16. E[LBOGEN], I[SMAR]. Schechter, Salomon
Schne'ur. (*In* Jüdisches Lexikon. *Berlin*, [1930].
Bd. 4, [pt.] 2, cols. 163–165.)

17. GIBSON, MARGARET. Dr Solomon Schechter.
(*Weekday*, Jan. 15, 1916.)

18. GINZBERG, LOUIS. Solomon Schechter. [An address delivered at the Schechter memorial exercises of
the J.T.S.A., Jan. 3, 1916.] (*Am. Heb.* vol. 98, 1915–
16, pp. 269–270.)

18*a*. —— —— *New York*, 1916. 12 pp. Nar.
16°.
Repr. *Am. Heb.*

18*b*. —— —— (*In his* Students, scholars and
saints. *Philadelphia*, 1928. Pp. 241–251. 8°.)

19. GREENSTONE, JULIUS H. Schechter, Solomon.
(*In* Encyclopaedia of the Social Sciences. *New York*,
1924. Vol. 13, pp. 565–566.)

20. HALPERN, ABRAHAM E. Professor Schechter—
the master mind. [Portrait.] (*Jewish Voice*. St Louis,
1919. Vol. 67, no. 26, pp. 1, 8.)

21. HEBREW UNION COLLEGE MONTHLY. Solomon
Schechter. [Portrait.] (Vol. 2, no. 4, Jan. 1916.)

Contents: E. L. Heinsheimer, Remarks [delivered at
the memorial service held at the H.U.C., Dec. 18, 1915].
K. Kohler, Solomon Schechter; memorial address. D. Philipson,
Solomon Schechter. Resolutions by the Faculty and the Board

of Governors [also in *Am. Heb.* vol. 98, p. 249]. Editorial: Memoria in aeterna! [by S. J. Abrams]. J. Bloch, Solomon Schechter: the scholar. A. S. Oko, Bibliography of Solomon Schechter: Preface [only].

22. HIRSCH, EMIL GUSTAV. Scholarship and Jewish theology. [Address delivered at the Judaean banquet in honor of S., May 29, 1902.] (*Am. Heb.* vol. 71, 1902, pp. 159–160.)
From the *Reform Advocate.*

22 *a.* —— Dr Schechter and Jewish scholarship in America. (*In* Judaean addresses. *New York*, 1917. Vol. 2, pp. 23–26. 8°.)

23. JACOBS, JOSEPH. Professor Solomon Schechter. [Portrait.] (*Am. Heb.* vol. 82, 1907–8, pp. 121–124.)
Written on the occasion of S.'s sixtieth birthday.

24. JEWISH CHRONICLE. Dr Schechter. [Editorial comment, and reference to his operation.] (Oct. 16, 1914, p. 5.)

25. —— Some tributes [by J. H. Hertz, M. Gaster, Morris Joseph, and Israel I. Mattuck]. Vote of sympathy by the Council of the United Synagogue of England. Obituary notice from the *Manchester Guardian.* (Nov. 26, 1915, pp. 23–24.)

26. JEWISH COMMENT. The Faculty of the Jewish Theological Seminary of America. [Personal sketches.] (Vol. 19, 1904, no. 8, pp. 1–4.)

27. JEWISH THEOLOGICAL SEMINARY OF AMERICA. זכר צדיק לברכה. Memorial exercises in memory of Solomon Schechter....Monday evening, January 3, 1916, Aeolian Hall, New York. [*New York*, 1916.] 19 pp. 8°.
See also *Am. Heb.* vol. 98, 1916, p. 241 (report of meeting and speeches).

28. —— Memorial addresses [by Alexander Marx and Sol M. Strook] delivered on the occasion of the second anniversary of the death of Dr Solomon Schechter, November 26th, 1917, at the Jewish Theological Seminary of America. [*New York*, 1917.] 10 pp., 1 l. [blank]. 8°.
Title from paper-cover.

29. JEWISH THEOLOGICAL SEMINARY OF AMERICA STUDENTS' ANNUAL. Schechter memorial. [Plates and Portraits.] (Vol. 3, 1916.)

Contents: A dirge by R. Solomon Ibn Gabirol [tr. from the Hebrew by Abraham Burnstein; sung in Hebrew by the students at the memorial service]. Dedication. Foreword [by Solomon Goldman]. Letters [to S., in Hebrew] from I. H. Weiss: [1. Testimonial, 1879; 2. Letter and testimonial from M. Friedmann, 1879]. Zeugniss from I. H. Weiss and M. Friedman[n; endorsed also by A. Jellinek, Oct. 5, 1876]. Empfehlung from Dr Jellinek [April 28, 1879]. Lovingkindness and truth, by S. Schechter. Excerpts from Dr Schechter's "Studies in Judaism". Excerpts from "Some aspects of rabbinic theology". Excerpts from "Seminary addresses and other papers". Teacher and friend, by Moses J. S. Abels. A true Jewish scholar, by Herman Abramowitz. Solomon Solis Cohen's tribute. Solomon Schechter, by Harry Friedenwald. Dr Schechter as scholar, by Louis Ginzberg. Memorial address, by Julius H. Greenstone. The Chief Rabbi's [J. H. Hertz] Schechter memorial address. Appreciation of Dr Schechter, by Joseph Hevesh. The master workman, by Charles I. Hoffman. Solomon Schechter as scholar and as man, by Joseph Jacobs. Some aspects of Schechter, by Joseph Jacobs. Solomon Schechter, by Kaufman[n] Kohler. Dr Schechter as Jew and theologian, by Eugene Kohn. A student's tribute to Dr Schechter, by Herman Lissauer. Solomon Schechter, by Louis Marshall. An appreciation, by J. S. Minkin. Dr Schechter's grave, by A. A. Neuman. Solomon Schechter, by David Philipson. Address, by H. H. Rubenowitz. E. Solomon's Eulogy at the funeral. Solomon Schechter, by Samuel Strauss. Israel's debt to Schechter, by Jacob H. Schiff. Mayer Sulzberger's Address. Editorials from "The American Hebrew" ["Schechter in America"

SOLOMON SCHECHTER

(Nov. 26, 1915); "Schechter's theology" (by J. Jacobs), a criticism of I. Zangwill's interview]. Resolutions: [Faculty of J.T.S.A.; Morais Blumenthal Society; Faculty of Hebrew Union College; Board of Governors of H.U.C.; J.P.S.A.]. Tributes: [Louis Marshall; Mayer Sulzberger; Cyrus Adler; K. Kohler; Jacob H. Schiff; Samuel Schulman; Francis Brown; Joseph Silverman; John H. Finley; Nicholas Murray Butler; Elmer Ellsworth Brown; Joseph H. Hertz; Adolph Lewisohn].

30. JEWISH YEAR BOOK. Schechter, Solomon. (5659. London, 1898. Pp. 208–209.)

31. KOHLER, KAUFMAN[N]. Solomon Schechter. [Memorial address delivered at the Chapel of the Hebrew Union College, Dec. 18, 1915.] (*In his* Hebrew Union College and other addresses. *Cincinnati*, 1916. Pp. 323–336. 8°.)

32. KOHUT, GEORGE ALEXANDER. Sonnet to Solomon Schechter. (*In* Friedlander, Joseph. Standard book of Jewish verse. *New York*, 1917. Pp. 736. 12°.)

"Suggested by Professor Schechter's luminous epistle on 'Spiritual Religion'."

33. [LEVIN, LOUIS H. (?).] Thumb-nail sketches of noted Jews. III. Solomon Schechter. [Portrait.] (*J. Comment*, vol. 16, 1902–3, no. 1, pp. 4–5.)

34. L[IPKIND], G[OODMAN]. Schechter, Solomon. (*In* Jewish Encyclopedia, vol. 11, pp. 93–94.)

35. LIPSKY, LOUIS. Death of Dr Schechter. (*Yiddishe, Dos, Folk* [English department]. New York, 1915. Vol. 1, no. 46.)

36. M[   ], B. Schechter, Shneiur Zalman. (*In* Ozar Yisrael: an encyclopedia [Hebrew]. *New York*, 1913. Vol. 10, pp. 196–197.)

APPENDIX

37. MARGOLIS, MAX L., and MARX, A. Solomon Schechter. (*In their* A history of the Jewish people. *Philadelphia*, 1927. Pp. 722–723. 8°.)

38. MARSHALL, LOUIS. Solomon Schechter. [Address delivered at the memorial meeting, Jan. 3, 1916, Aeolian Hall.] (*Am. Heb.* vol. 98, 1916, pp. 242–244.)

38 *a*. —— —— (*American Israelite* [Cincinnati], vol. 62, Jan. 13, 1916, p. 1.)

39. MARX, ALEXANDER. Solomon Schechter. (*In* American Jewish Historical Society. Publications. [*Baltimore*], 1917. No. 25, pp. 177–192. 8°.)

39 *a*. —— —— [*Baltimore*, 1917.] 16 pp. 8°. Repr. *Am. Jewish Hist. Soc. Publ.*

40. MOORE, GEORGE FOOTE. Schechter: scholar and humanist. [Portrait.] (*Menorah Journal.* New York, 1916. Vol. 2, pp. 1–6.)

41. NACHT, J[ACOB]. Biografie. (*In* Schechter, S., Chassidimi....Traducere de B. Zosmer. Cu o biografie a autorului de J. Nacht. [*Bucreşti*], 1910. Pp. ? 16°.)
See also his "The Jews of Rumania" [Hebrew], in *Hashiloah*, vol. 17, pp. 545 ff.

42. NEW INTERNATIONAL ENCYCLOPAEDIA. Schechter, Solomon. (*New York*, 1910. Vol. 17, p. 650.)

43. NEW YORK, N.Y. KEHILATH ISRAEL SYNAGOGUE. Dedicatory exercises in connection with the unveiling of a memorial tablet in honor of Solomon Schechter, President of the Jewish Theological Seminary of America....Sunday afternoon, Jan. 14, 1917, [at] Kehilath Israel Synagogue...New York. [*New York*, 1917.] 4 l. [last blank]. 8°.

44. PHILIPSON, DAVID. Solomon Schechter. (*American Israelite* [Cincinnati], vol. 62, no. 26.)

45. Schiff, Jacob Henry. [Introductory address at the memorial meeting, Jan. 3, 1916, Aeolian Hall.] (*Am. Heb.* vol. 98, 1916, p. 241.)

46. Schulman, Samuel. The genius of Solomon Schechter. (*Am. Heb.* vol. 99, 1916, pp. 688, 734.)

46a. —— In memory of Solomon Schechter. (*In* Central Conference of American Rabbis. Yearbook. [*Cincinnati, O.*, 1916.] Pp. 218–223. 8°.)

47. Silberbusch, David Isaiah. Reminiscences on [!] Solomon Schechter. [Hebrew.] (*Rimon*. Berlin, 1924. No. 6, pp. 31–36.)
Same in Yiddish edition of *Rimon*.

48. Singer, Isidore. Professor Schechter's message to the Jews of America. (*New Era*. New York, 1904. Vol. 5, no. 5, pp. 480–491.)
Criticism of S.'s theological position and religious policy. Advance publication in *Reform Advocate*. See also *J.C.* Dec. 30, 1904, p. 21.

49. Solomon, Elias L. Solomon Schechter: master builder. [Portrait.] (*J. Exponent*, vol. 70, no. 10, 1919, pp. 1, 8.)
See also p. 4: "The method of Schechter" (editorial).

50. Yiddishe, Dos, Folk [New York]. Prof. Shlomeh Schechter geshtorben. (Vol. 7, no. 47, Nov. 26, 1915, pp. 1, 3.)
See also English department ("Resolution on death of Dr Schechter"). From *Yiddishe Literatur un Geshichte*.

51. Zangwill, Israel. Send-off to Dr Schechter [on taking up the headship of the J.T.S.A., April 1902.] (*In his* Speeches, articles and letters. *London*, 1937. Pp. 64–74. 8°.)

52. ZANGWILL, ISRAEL. [Tribute to S.; interview. Portrait.] (*Am. Heb.* vol. 98, 1916, p. 240.)

Z. also refers to S. in his "The position of Judaism" (*North American Review*, 1895; see also *J.C.* April 19, 1895, p. 11); and in his "Light from the East" (*Cosmopolitan*, Sept. 1896; also *Reform Advocate*) he comments on S.'s writings.

II

NOTICES AND REFERENCES

1. CAMBRIDGE UNIVERSITY

53. Mr S. Schechter and Cambridge University. [Conferment of M.A. degree, *h.c.*, May 12, 1892.] (*J.C.* May 13, 1892, p. 18.)

54. DULBERG, JOSEPH. Mr S. Schechter and Cambridge University. [Letter to editor; with reference to the M.A. degree.] (*J.C.* May 27, 1892, pp. 12–13.)

55. Mr S. Schechter and Cambridge University. [Grant of Worts Scholarship of £100 to visit Italian libraries.] (*J.C.* Nov. 25, 1892, p. 17.)

56. Mr S. Schechter and Cambridge University. Conferment of a Doctor's degree. [Portrait.] (*J.C.* Feb. 11, 1898, p. 12.)

See also p. 19 (editorial comment). Repr. *Reform Advocate*, vol. 15, p. 100.

57. [Reference to S. in connection with other Cambridge tutors.] (*J.C.* Jan. 27, 1893, p. 6.)

58. [Subjects of lectures by S. during the first and second terms, 1893–94.] (*J.C.* Oct. 22, 1893, p. 14.)

59. An Oxford and Cambridge night at the Maccabaeans. [The influence of S.] (*J.C.* Dec. 22, 1899, pp. 14–15.)

See also *Oesterreichische Wochenschrift*, Jahrg. 16, p. 118.

60. Professor Schechter and the University of Cambridge. [Communication of General Board of Studies to Special Board of Oriental Studies of Cambridge University with regard to his call to America.] (*J.C.* Feb. 9, 1900, p. 14.)

61. Dr Schechter's successor [I. Abrahams; editorial comment.] (*J.C.* March 21, 1902, p. 19.)

62. [Influence of S.'s work; editorial note.] (*Am. Heb.* vol. 71, 1902, p. 631.)

2. ITALY. GENIZAH. UNIVERSITY COLLEGE, LONDON

63. [Postponement of journey to Italy.] (*J.C.* Dec. 30, 1892, p. 15.)

64. [Travel on the Continent.] (*J.C.* June 23, 1893, p. 13.)

65. [Return to England.] (*J.C.* Aug. 4, 1893, p. 10.)

66. [Journey to Palestine, after completing work at Cairo.] (*J.C.* Feb. 19, 1897, p. 23.)

67. Mr Schechter's return. The "Geniza". [Editorial comments.] (*J.C.* April 2, 1897, pp. 19–20.)

68. The Hebrew MSS. from the Cairo Genizah. [Report of the Library Syndicate of Cambridge University on the offer made by C. Taylor and S.] (*J.C.* June 17, 1898, p. 19.)

69. The MS. treasures of the Cairo Geniza. [Translation of official Latin letters of thanks from J. E. Sandys to C. Taylor and S. for presenting collection to Cambridge University.] (*J.C.* Dec. 30, 1898, p. 12.)

See also *J.C.* Jan. 28, 1898, p. 25; June 1, 1900, p. 32; May 20, 1910, p. 18, and July 1, p. 22.

70. The Hebrew professorship at University College. "Call" to Dr Schechter [to the Goldsmid professorship]. (*J.C.* Dec. 9, 1898, p. 9.)

71. Professor Schechter. [Motion by the Cambridge Hebrew Congregation to extend congratulations to S. on his appointment to the Goldsmid professorship.] (*J.C.* Dec. 16, 1898, p. 12.)

72. Dinner to Professor Schechter [by the Maccabeans upon his appointment to the Goldsmid professorship; editorial comment]. (*J.C.* Feb. 3, 1899, p. 18.)

3. JEWISH THEOLOGICAL SEMINARY OF AMERICA

73. A "call" for Professor Schechter. (*J.C.* Oct. 20, 1899, p. 13.)

74. Dr Schechter's "call" to America. [Comment; from *J. Exponent.*] (*J.C.* Nov. 10, 1899, p. 26.)

75. Prof. S. Schechter and the New York Seminary. [Denial of authenticity of call; and comment from *Reform Advocate.*] (*J.C.* Jan. 5, 1900, p. 9.)

76. Professor Schechter and the New York Jewry. [Its lack of interest in furthering call.] (*J.C.* March 2, 1900, p. 25.)

77. Dr Schechter and the Seminary. [Editorial comments.] (*Am. Heb.* vol. 70, 1901–2, pp. 132–133.)

78. The coming of Dr Schechter. [Opinions culled from the Jewish press.] (*Am. Heb.* vol. 70, 1901–2, pp. 196–197, 220.)

79. Greetings to Doctor Schechter. [Editorial.] (*Am. Heb.* vol. 70, 1901–2, p. 656.)

80. Endowment of the Seminary. [S. to secure a Faculty that will equal in scholarship any institution of learning.] (*Am. Heb.* vol. 71, 1902, p. 124.)

81. American problems and solutions. [Reference to the "vigorous and already famous 'orthodox' Seminary presided over by Dr Schechter".] (*J.C.* May 27, 1904, p. 22.)

82. The Theological Seminary in New York. [Letter to the editor by "A (Portuguese) Founder of the Old Seminary" (Henry S. Morais?), taking exception to remark by Baltimore correspondent (*J.C.* June 24, 1904, p. 27) that "in Jewish scholarship there is no such thing as orthodoxy or reform".] (*J.C.* July 22, 1904, p. 19.)
See also Aug. 26, p. 15 (reply).

83. Jottings from the United States. [Reference to criticism by Orthodox Union of Rabbis of "Schechter's institution": S. not being orthodox enough.] (*J.C.* Aug. 12, 1904, p. 20.)

84. [Comment on S.'s toast: "The J.T.S.A.", at meeting of J.P.S.A.] (*J. Comment*, vol. 19, 1904, no. 7, p. 12.)

85. The scope of the Seminary. [Editorial comment on S.'s conception of what it ought to be.] (*Am. Heb.* vol. 78, 1905–6, pp. 539–540.)

APPENDIX

86. The Jewish Theological Seminary in New York. [Baltimore correspondent appraises value of institution to American Judaism since S.'s incumbency.] (*J.C.* Oct. 19, 1906, p. 19.)

87. [Reference to address at meeting of Alumni Association of J.T.S.A.] (*J.C.* July 17, 1908, p. 12.)

4. MISCELLANEOUS

88. [Appointed by Council of Jews' College to direct a class twice a week in Talmudical subjects; editorial comment.] (*J. Standard*, Oct. 2, 1888, pp. 6–7.)

89. Jews' College Literary Society. [Report of meeting presided over by S.] (*J.C.* Dec. 19, 1890, p. 15.)

90. [Elected member of Society of Historical Theology, Oxford; S. being one of three Jewish members.] (*J.C.* June 29, 1894, p. 18.)
See *J.C.* Jan. 26, 1894, p. 14. ("Mr Schechter has promised a paper on the 'Miracles of Rabbis'. This ought to be interesting.")

91. [J. Jacobs' "Studies in Biblical archaeology" dedicated to S.] (*J.C.* Oct. 19, 1894, p. 15.)

92. [Dr and Mrs S. attend dedication of Semitic Museum of Harvard University.] (*J.C.* Feb. 27, 1903, p. 23.)

93. Prof. Schechter in New York University Senate. [Appointed as representative of Faculty of J.T.S.A.] (*J. Comment*, vol. 18, 1903–4, no. 7, p. 11.)

94. [Elected member of Publication Committee of J.P.S.A.] (*J. Comment*, vol. 18, 1903–4, no. 19, p. 6.)

95. Jottings from the United States. [Announcement of course of lectures on the "Wisdom of Ben Sirah" before the Jewish Chautauqua Assembly at Atlantic City.] (*J.C.* July 22, 1904, p. 22.)

96. [Elected member of Council of International Society of the Apocrypha; the other two Jews on the Council being M. Gaster and I. Lévi.] (*J.C.* July 5, 1907, p. 25.)

97. [Receives his U.S. naturalization papers.] (*J.C.* July 3, 1908, p. 13.)

98. [Harvard University confers upon S. honorary degree of Doctor of Letters; the first Jew to receive this distinction. Elected head of the newly organized Union of Orthodox Rabbis and Congregations.] (*J.C.* Sept. 22, 1911 [New Year supplement], p. xv.)

See also *Harvard Graduate Magazine*, vol. 20, no. 77.

ADDENDA

1897

ABRAHAMS, ISRAEL. Jewish life in the middle ages. *London* [also *Philadelphia*], 1896. 8°. [Review of.] (*Critical Review of Theological & Philosophical Literature*, vol. 7, 1897, pp. 16–21.)

To no. 87 (Reviews)

[ANONYMOUS.] Reviews and notices. (*Imperial and Asiatic Quarterly Review and Oriental and Colonial Record*, ser. 3, vol. 2, 1896, p. 443.)

BENN, A. W. [Review.] (*Academy* [London], vol. 50, 1896, p. 174.)

SKINNER, J. [Review.] (*Critical Review of Theological & Philosophical Literature*, vol. 6, 1896, pp. 367–370.)

To no. 89 (Reviews)

G[ASTER], M. Notices of books. (*Journal of the Royal Society of Great Britain and Ireland*, 1896, pp. 644–646.)

STRACK, H. L. [Review.] (*Theologisches Literaturblatt*, 1898, cols. 209 f.)

To no. 102

Finds in the Cairo Genizah. (*Sunday-school Times*. Philadelphia, 1898. Vol. 40, pp. 163 f.)

Spoils from a Jewish Genizah. (*Independent* [New York], vol. 49, 1898, p. 1429.)

To no. 107 (Reviews)

FELL, W. [Review.] (*Literarische Rundschau für das Katholische Deutschland*, 1900, pp. 329–331.)

HALÉVY, J. Bibliographie. (*Revue Sémitique*, année 7, 1899, pp. 370–372.)

R[YSSEL]. [Review.] (*Literarisches Zentralblatt*, Jahrg. 51, 1900, cols. 1689–1692.)

STRACK, H. L. [Review.] (*Theologisches Literaturblatt*, 1899, cols. 537–540.)

ADDENDA

To no. 137 (Note and Review)

The "Addenda et corrigenda" (pp. 773–825) were compiled by M. Berlin.

[Anonymous review.] (*Athenaeum* [London], Sept. 5, 1903, p. 312.)

To no. 165 (III)

"Prof. Dr Büchler kindly drew my attention [to it] some years ago, and prepared a copy for me."

To no. 182 (Note)

"In Appendix A are published, for the first time, from Manuscripts, four lists of moral precepts...composed by R. Moses Cordovero, Abraham Galanti, Abraham Halevi, and Moses of Lieria (?)." List 1, from MS. Columbia University Library: C 812, X 893 (entitled *Likkute Shoshanim*); 2, 3 and 4 from a MS. in the Library of the J.T.S.A.

To Appendix (I)

A[DLER], C[YRUS]. Schechter, Solomon. (*In* Dictionary of American biography. *New York.* [1935]. Vol. 16, pp. 421–423.)

AHAD HAAM, *pseud.* of A. Ginzberg. [Letters to S.; 1906–13.] (*In his* אגרות. *Tel-Aviv*, 1924–25. 8°. Vol. 3, pp. 255–256; Vol. 4, pp. 24–25, 46–47, 223, 255–258; vol. 5, pp. 21–22, 90–93, 105–106.)

References to S., vol. 5, pp. 100 and 104.

DEINARD, EPHRAIM. [References to S.] (*In his* זכרונות בת עמי. *St Louis*, [1920]. 8°. Vol. 2, pp. 42, 142–146.)

See also his animadversion on S. in his Catalogue of the M. Sulzberger Library (אור מאיר, *New York*, 1896, p. 20, no. 9.) According to D., Sulzberger had on that account that leaf removed from most of the copies.

94

INDEX

Bevan, A. A., 107 r
Bible (J.P.S.A.), 224, 236
  Canon, 72
  Criticism, 110–110a, 136, 151–151b. *See also* Ecclesiastes; Ecclesiasticus; Pentateuch
Blau, L., 195 r
Bloch, J., *A* 13–14a, 21
Bodleian Library, *see* Manuscripts (Oxford)
Boehl, F. M. T., 195 r
Books, Hebrew, *see* Hebrew books
Bosniak, J., 238
Bousset, W., 195 r
Box, C. H., 188 r [note]
British Museum, 32–32b. *See also* Manuscripts
Broch, I., 54b
Brown, E. E., *A* 29
Brown, F., *A* 29
Bruell, N., 14 r, 40a
Buber, S., 86, 92
Buchanan, C., 77
Budde, K., 90a r
Buechler, A., 195 r, 228, *Ad* [to 165]
Burnstein, A., *A* 29
Butler, N. M., *A* 29

Cairo Genizah, *see* Genizah
Cambridge (Eng.)—Hebrew Congregation, 103, *A* 71
Cambridge Review, *A* 15
Cambridge University, 40–40a, 142, *A* 53–62. *See also* Genizah; Manuscripts
Chajes, H. P., 195 r
Chamiz, *see* Ḥamiz
Charles, R. H., 195 r
Cheyne, T. K., 40–40a
Child, The, 47–47a
Chotzner, J., 7, 128 n
Christianity and Judaism, *see* Judaism
Chushiel, *see* Hushiel
Cincinnati, O., 227
Clark, T. and T. (Publishers), 188 n
Cohen, L., 32b, 45 n
Cohen, S. Solis-, *see* Solis-Cohen
Columbia University, *see* Manuscripts

Commentary to Moed Katon, *see* Moed Katon
  to the Passover Haggadah, *see* Haggadah shel Pesaḥ
  to the 13 Rules of Interpretation, *see* Middot
Cordovero, Moses, *Ad* [to 182]
Correspondence, *see* Letters
Cowen, P., 240
Cowley, A. E., 137 r
Critic, 87 r

Daiches, S., 195 r
Damascus, *see* Zadokite Sect
David Hannasi, Karaite, 135
David Messer Léon, *see* Léon
Davidson, I., 1 n, 2 n, 136 n, 239
Davies, I. W., 182 r, 188 r
Dedications, 4, 7, 11, 14, 17a, 87, 89, 128, 137, 156, 178, 182, 185, 195, 221
De Haas, J., 168 n
Deinard, E., *Ad* [to *A*, I]
Dembitzer, H. N., 52
De Rossi, G. B., *see* Manuscripts (Parma)
Divine retribution, *see* Retribution
Dobsevage, I. G., 238
Doctor, degree of, *A* 52, 98
Dods, M., 87 r
Dogmas, 39–39a
Driver, S. R., 40–40a
Dropsie College, 202–202a, 211–211b
Dukes, L., 56
Dulberg, J., *A* 54

Ecclesiastes, 10
Ecclesiasticus, 59, 90–90a, 97, 101, 105, 107–110a, 115–119, 123, 128, 130, 172, *A* 95
Edersheim, A., 9–9a
Education, religious, 179–179b
Egypt, 114–114a. *See also* Fostat
Eisler, R., 195 r
Elbogen, I., 231 r, *A* 16
Elegy, *see* Kinah
Elijah ha-Kohen b. Abraham, 150–150a
Elijah Wilna, 45–45d

Ellinger, M., 87 r
Emden, Jacob, 24–24 a
England, Jews in, *see* Great Britain
  Jewish literature in, *see* Jewish
    literature
  Rabbis of, *see* Great Britain
  translation of the Talmud in, *see*
    Talmud
Ethnography, 3
Europe, Jews in, 205–205 b
European War, 1914–1918, 235–235 c
Evasion Laws, *see* Legal evasions

Falk, H. S. J., 24–24 a
Fell, W., *Ad* [to 107]
Finley, J. H., *A* 29
Foakes-Jackson, F. J., 195 r
Folk-tales, 33, 41–42
Fostat, 150–150 a
Four Captives, The, 113
Francis of Assisi, 61 n
Frankfurter Zeitung, 195 r
Frankl, P. F., 17 a, 87
Freudenthal, J., 40–40 a
Friedenberg, A. M., 131 n, 145–146
Friedenwald, H., *A* 29
Friedlaender, I., 236
Friedlaender, M., 10, 14 r
Friedlander, J., 182 r [note]
Friedmann, Baer, of Leovo, 2
Friedmann, M., 40 a, 134, 148,
  186–186 b, *A* 29

Galante, Abraham, *Ad* [to 182]
Galante, Moses, 29
Gaster, M., *A* 25, *Ad* [to 89]
Geiger, A., 238
Genizah, discovery and description
  of, 98–99, 102–102 a, 122, 138,
  202–202 a, *A* 66–69, *Ad* [to
  102]
  fragments from, 105–107, 113–
    114 a, 127, 130, 135–136, 147–
    148, 150–150 a, 165–166, 195,
    203–203 a, 214–215, 218–218 a,
    223–223 a
Geonim, 63
Germany, Jewish Saints in, *see*
  Saints
  Jews in, 182

Gibson, M., 90 n, *A* 17. *See also*
  Manuscripts (Lewis-Gibson)
Gilbert, G. H., 188 r
Ginzberg, Asher, *see* Ahad HaAm
Ginzberg, L., 137 r, 195 r, 203 a r,
  218 n, *A* 18–18 b, 29
Glueckel of Hameln, 182
Gnomic literature, 156, 165–165 a
Goldman, S., *A* 29
Goldsmid-Montefiore, C., *see* Monte-
  fiore
Goldziher, I., 147 r
Goodness, 104, 188 a
Gordon, H. Z., 232
Gornish, 25, 27, 29
Gottheil, R. J. H., 40 a, 136 r
Graetz, H., 19, 30, 40–40 a, 55,
  62–62 a
Gratz College, 81
Great Britain, Jews in, 25, 27, 56,
  76, 124–126, 132–132 b. *See
  also* United Synagogue of
  Great Britain
Green, A. L., 56
Greene, W. B., jr., 188 r
Greenstone, J. H., 218 n, *A* 19, 29
Gressmann, H., 195 r
Grimm, *Bros.*, 41
Guedemann, M., 30, 40 a

Haggadah, 43
Haggadah shel Pesaḥ, Commentary
  to, 64
Halberstam, S. J., 40 a, 69 n, 239
Halévy, J., *Ad* [to 107]
Halpern, A. E., *A* 20
Hamiz, Joseph, 71
Harkavy, A., 26, 156
Harper's Weekly, 197 r
Harris, Miriam, 47 n
Harvard University, 169, *A* 92, 98
Ḥasidism, 1–2, 17–17 e
Hastings, J., 87 r
Hebrew books, 32–32 b
  literature, 28
  manuscripts, *see* Manuscripts;
    Genizah
Hebrew Union College, 231
  Board of Governors, *A* 21, 29
  Faculty, *A* 21, 29

For EU product safety concerns, contact us at Calle de José Abascal, 56–1°,
28003 Madrid, Spain or eugpsr@cambridge.org.